THE STRUGGLE FOR PEACE

*The Story of Casualties Union
in the years following the
Second World War*

Also by Eric Claxton:

Practical Rescue Training (Pitman & Sons Ltd.)
Realistic Battle Training for Civil Defence (Gale
  & Polden Ltd.)
More Ways Than One of Fighting a War (The
  Book Guild Ltd.)
Hidden Stevenage (The Book Guild Ltd.)

The Struggle for Peace

*The Story of Casualties Union
in the years following the
Second World War*

Eric Claxton

Foreword by
Nancy Mortimer Budgett

The Book Guild Ltd.
Sussex, England

The Book Guild Ltd.
25 High Street,
Lewes, Sussex.

First published
© Eric Claxton 1992
Set in Baskerville
Typesetting by Hawks Typesetters, Horley, Surrey
Printed in Great Britain by
Antony Rowe Ltd.
Chippenham, Wiltshire.

A catalogue record for this book is
available from the British Library

ISBN 0 86332 719 2

I dedicate this book to all those who have served as acting responsive casualties or invalids for the rehearsal of new and traditional methods of treating and handling sick and injured persons in domestic, industrial and transport accidents.

CONTENTS

LIST OF ILLUSTRATIONS

ACKNOWLEDGEMENTS

I acknowledge the source of most of these reports of the activities of Casualties Union and its members through the years after the war as being extracts from *Casualties Union Journal* first published in 1946 to 1958, and later in a new-look format under the title *Casualty Simulation* from 1958 to 1985. I wish to express my thanks to each of the authors of the several items and especially to the editors.

The authors are far too numerous to mention individually, but I would like to thank the editors, John R. Stevens and Mrs Helen M. Nicholson. Both of them were active senior instructors and the literary burden was an extra, a special work of devotion.

Helen Nicholson started to assist John Stevens in 1951 and two years later towards the end of 1953, when John could no longer give the time to this essential service, she was able to take over the editorship and continued as editor for thirty-two years until the General Management Committee decided to cancel further issues. The union owes both of them a most special vote of thanks.

I hope that these items collated from those sources, with little more than the labour of copying being required from me, will be found acceptable and informative. Of necessity it can only be a modest selection and I apologize for having to leave out many excellent reports from the hand of worthy authors. I regret this but suggest that members are recommended to study the records of those important forty years.

Thank you, editors both, and contributors all, not forgetting the photographers. Thank you, Nancy Budgett, for your kindness in so willingly writing a foreword.

ERIC CLAXTON

FOREWORD

It is an honour and a great pleasure to contribute a few words of welcome to the saga of Casualties Union. This book follows up the wartime development of a special service, which members joined for many differing reasons — some because they experienced a sickening reaction after seeing a severely shocked and gory patient at a recruiting demonstration in 1942 and realizing their own inadequacies in coping with the needs of those with actual war injuries.

How quickly we learned the rudiments at Leatherhead Rescue School, and how much we gained by the experience of being handled. Then and ever since the founding of Casualties Union in 1942 members willingly gave their time and energy to follow Eric Claxton and Brenda Whiteley in their struggle, both during the war and in the so-called era of peace that followed. In return members gained for themselves much experience and personal friendships beyond all value.

Our thanks go to all those who served in the past; but the present extends before us with many changes, global eruptions, inventions, discoveries, and adventures, and simulated casualties will still be needed to help with the training of all the caring services.

This saga, in all its varied chapters, gives the story of a world wide service in the struggle for peace against the ravages of accidents at home, in the street, at sport, in industry and transport. I commend this book as an inspiration to all readers and, as each generation courageously hands on the torch, may it be remembered that 'All the flowers of all the tomorrows are in the seeds of TODAY'.

NANCY MORTIMER BUDGETT

'We were still surrounded by casualties of all kinds in every direction'

PREFACE

VE Day came amid rejoicing, but the training at the Rescue School at Leatherhead, still went on for the military destined for service in the Far East. VJ Day came and the fighting ceased even in the Far East theatre, so our duties of training the services ended; we pooled our skills and prepared for our final day at the Rescue School when the whole of Civil Defence stood down on 2 July 1945.

Some of us decided that our approach to learning and teaching how to approach, examine, diagnose, treat and extricate wartime casualties from bombed situations, applied, unfortunately, equally well to the casualties of peacetime. Our doctors pointed this out to us in no uncertain terms. One went so far as to tell us that if Casualties Union ceased to exist, he would feel obliged to create a similar organization to help fight the casualties occuring in peacetime in the homes, on the streets, on the playing fields, in industry and with transport of all kinds.

I felt that I had had more than enough, but together with those hundred odd members we ventured forth with this new mission that would have to be fitted into our leisure time. Faced with the accident statistics, there was no doubt that we were still surrounded by casualties of all kinds in all directions. There were lots of people willing to help, but they all needed experience — needed to make all their mistakes on us members of Casualties Union, whose responsive behaviour helped first aiders, rescuemen and nurses to learn how best to handle injured people. They needed to rehearse on us — there were a lot of them, if they would let us help them. Somehow we had to produce sufficient skilled casualties wherever people were eager to learn. It seemed an impossible task.

On 3 July 1945, the day following the standing down of Civil Defence and the final gathering of members at Surrey County Rescue School, Leatherhead, it was my grievous duty to dismantle the school premises with all its provocative challenges. They could never have been maintained in a satisfactory condition, while no longer in daily use, and it was essential that their former owners should have them restored to their former use as a convent school, or as residences, as the case might be. There was much of each.

The brave new Casualties Union was left with nothing; just some 100 members, with their personal talents, financial resources and limited spare time. We each needed to earn a living, and those who had been seconded to Civil Defence were called back to their former work.

I duly reported back to Surrey County Hall, Kingston-upon-Thames, to discover that with bomb damage and many other changes, there was no place for me — I was to be lodged in an upper room of a semi-detached house nearby. Worse still, of course, there was no creative work for me to do. It would take time for the wheels of peacetime to begin to turn.

Nevertheless, some things moved quickly in those days. My former college pal, who had been best man at my wedding in 1935, Captain R.H.P. Barter, RE, had been a prisoner of war in Germany ever since his part of the retreat from Dunkirk had failed. He visited me and we spent a happy day together. He must have been interested in some of my experiences, and mentioned them to a college acquaintance, who within ten days of my return to the office, phoned me.

Without preamble, he said: 'Eric, what about building a New Town?' I was desperate to get back to building bridges and I was not really interested in being an urban engineer, yet I knew in a flash, that this New Town was what all my previous experience had been preparing me to undertake. I expect that I replied, 'Yes!'

He continued: 'If you are interested, get in touch with Professor Holford, Director of Planning Techniques at the Ministry of Town and Country Planning.'

I took up the challenge and went to see Professor Holford. He seemed to think that it was a good idea for me to join the team and, although nobody else agreed, I was engineer to the project from that moment.

In the first instance I was to be seconded to the Ministry of Town and Country Planning for a year, but my employers refused to consider it. It took some six months before I was allowed to go for six months. After playing my part in preparing a plan for a New Town for 60,000 inhabitants at Stevenage, Hertfordshire, my secondment was extended for a further six months, by the end of which the New Town of Stevenage was designated. My employers refused to extend the secondment, but by then I was hooked on my New Town project and the county council generously extended my secondment for a final three months.

When I went to Stevenage Development Corporation to seek an appointment to continue my work, they had no use for a chap like me, but I stayed and made myself useful, meanwhile they paid me little more than a pittance. The first New Town was a touchy business politically and although I stayed until I retired 25 years later, it was then, and only then for the first time, that I felt my job was secure.

I hope I have not made too much of these personal problems, but they did complicate the activities of my duties as honorary organizer appointed to the new organization, which they had decided once more should be known as Casualties Union.

Eric C. Claxton

I

Dramatis Personae

To recall the events would have been beyond my memory, but I have been fortunate to retain copies of *The Journal of Casualties Union* over the years and I have unhesitatingly chosen articles published in it from the pens of many writers who together seem to have captured the story of Casualties Union.

The membership had been fortunate to be able to appoint such a widely experienced group of officers, who were not only generous with their knowledge but also with their personal and private resources. John Loarridge, ACA, honorary secretary, who allowed us to use his offices in Bedford Row, London WC1; the honorary treasurer, C.J.M. Adie, MA, a retired housemaster at Eton College, used his good offices to obtain permission to hold our first post war reunion on Fellow's Eyot at Eton College. Percy Sargeant, appeals secretary for a missionary society, willingly undertook the responsibilities of honorary appeals secretary.

John Stevens, MA, master of English at Cranleigh School, most helpfully agreed to become honorary editor of *Casualties Union Journal* — and I should add of everything else we were to publish during the early years. Sidney Francis, AIBP, was a professional photographer, who undertook to create a photographic record, and insisted on being honorary photographer, an appointment that must have been one of sheer generosity and professional brilliance. Whenever Sidney was personally involved in the event, his assistant was there with her camera — often both of them were making records.

The committee included Dr Millicent Pam, MB, BS, (Lond), and Doris Hammer who between them had invented and developed the practise of diagnosis, one of the remarkable bi-products of Casualties Union technique, since diagnosis could not previously be undertaken except with actual sick or injured persons, and certainly not in situations of disaster. The other members of the committee were Wilfred Davies, MInstM&CyE, FSI, surveyor to Chertsey UDC, Roy Stokes, BEM, foreman in a printing works, Captain Roland Lovesy, formerly OC Rescue School, and Lanta Spurrier the artist.

They soon divided into a number of sub-committees with special duties — most notably to foster publicity, finance and research. We were fortunate also to have some distinguished honorary medical advisers to whom we could refer, Dr J.E. Haine, MB, ChB, DPH, Guildford RDC's MOH; L.S. Michaelis, MD, Orthopaedic Surgeon at Stoke Manderville Hospital; Clive Shields, BM, BCh, MRCS, LRCP; Lieutenant-Colonel E.S. Goss, MC, MRCS(Eng), LRCP(Lond).

Clearly we had a splendid team.

2

Publicity

Publicity was urgent if the voluntary services offered by Casualties Union were to become known to potential users in the post-war world, quite apart form the need to keep in touch with our small existing membership. A journal was, we thought, essential, but no sooner had the editor gathered material than paper rationing controls vetoed a new periodical. We could, however, have an ad hoc one-off leaflet, so we devised 'Notes for the guidance of members'. I was lucky enough to retain a proof copy. Not surprisingly all the rest have gone, because in the circumstances that same issue had to serve also as our publicity material.

We started quite blatantly with these words: 'Peacetime is not a period of safety. It is true that shells, bombs, mines and other hazards of war are not present, but even so 1,000 persons are injured every day in this country'. There was no need to make any further case for the continued existence of Casualties Union.

A research sub-committee was set up under the chairmanship of Mrs Whiteley. The problems were legion. Wartime casualties had always been covered in dust and dirt, which helped to mask some of the imperfections in our make-up. For some naive reasons we were expecting to find the wounds of peacetime to be clean. In any case they turned out to be different. That sub-committee would never complete its task, because almost every request for our services brought new problems.

We had already had, in May 1945, at short notice, a request to provide a casualty for the final stage of a Metropolitan Police competition to be held at MacNaughton House, Euston. There were six teams, and the contest was carried out under St John rules. The 'casualty' had been dismantling a Morrison shelter (a metal table with four legs and able to shelter a young family) and was inside it when he sustained the following injuries:

- Broken jaw.
- Bleeding tongue. (Produced by cellulose paint which adheres for about twenty minutes and then peels off like a clot of blood. The tongue had to be dried with a cloth before application.)
- Simple fracture of elbow.
- Bruised leg.
- Concussion without complete loss of consciousness.

There were two problems. Although well staged for competitiors and judges, the spectators were unable to see much because competitors blocked the view. Also touching up the 'casualty's' injuries took rather longer than desirable for such competitions.

Six weeks later we were invited back to MacNaughton House. Duplicated 'casualties' were provided to avoid delays between relays of competitors, and the staging was arranged to give a better view to spectators. The 'problem' on this occasion took the form of a workman who had fallen from scaffolding, breaking his thigh and slashing the artery just above the elbow on a nail as he fell. The second injury was largely concealed since the workman was wearing a jacket which was only slightly torn by the nail. Nevertheless severe bleeding will always create problems for the make-up team.

The Boy Scout Association also made early demands upon our services and we were invited to give a demonstration to Rover Scouts in camp at Polyapes, Oxshott. This was interesting and we began to make useful friends and in particular were able to exhibit our talents and intentions before our new president, the eminent surgeon, Brigadier W. Rowley Bristow.

The British Red Cross Society invited us to give a demonstration to thirty instructors of its Surrey county branch on the playing fields of St John's School, Leatherhead, which were very near to the former Rescue School. It was not possible to prepare the site beforehand, so this occasion showed clearly that Casualties Union could undertake its work anywhere. Home, factory and road accidents were all able to be included in realistic settings and we were able to conclude with a difficult diagnosis exercise appropriate to the status and experience of our audience.

The Boy Scouts Association then paid us the tremendous compliment of inviting us to demonstrate at Gilwell Park on the occasion of the first reunion of Wood Badge holders since the outbreak of war. It took place in the presence of Lord Rowallan, the Chief Scout, John Thurman, the Camp Chief, Commissioners, Field Commissioners and several hundred Scouters.

The programme took the form of an illustrated talk, given by the organizer, in the sunken camp fire circle, and attempted to show how situations could be built up to give real experience of handling wounded people, and how it could be applied to Scouting in the four stages of training — Second Class, First Class, Ambulance Man, and Scouters and Rovers.

The Chief Scout was interested and I had the opportunity of asking whether he would consider becoming one of our vice-presidents. He accepted, and in due course took up office, which he retained until he was apppointed Governor of Canada.

There were twenty-one members in the party that went to Gilwell Park. All of them were in Civil Defence; most of them were in either the Red Cross or St John, but it is interesting to note that seven of the twenty-one were, or had been, warrant holders in the Scouting or Guiding movements. Perhaps this explains more clearly why, over the years, I have always found the members of Casualties Union to be special people — always ready to put others before themselves.

We were anxious to ensure that our standard was as high as we could reach and so in that hectic autumn we managed to run an instructors' course coupled with a refresher course at Millmead, Guildford, over two consecutive weekends in October 1945. One small incident remains in my memory from that occasion. We included a case of drowning in the River Way, hard by. Brenda was in the river keeping herself in position, ready to do her drowning act when the rescuers hove in sight. An elderly gentleman came wandering by.

'What's she doing in the water', he asked.

'Waiting to be rescued from drowning', I replied.

'What a stupid woman', was his final comment as he passed on his way. Brenda was duly rescued and lived to tell the tale.

3

Brochure

We needed help in high places and the publicity sub-committee considered that a glossy brochure would be valuable if it could be dropped discretely onto the right desks. Doris Hammer, the chairman, picked and chose and a number of us went scurrying here and there, while Sidney Francis took studio photographs in the most unlikely places.

We were anxious to encourage accident prevention as well as enlightened and realistic instruction and practice. We wanted to show something of the scope of peacetime accidents and how, by understanding the causation of disaster, they could be eliminated. The story is told with the minimal number of words and a series of eloquent photographs. Wherever the detail appears to be essential to the understanding of the special point to be made, an inset photo shows that detail.

There were fives sections entitled — BRCS and SJAB; YOUTH ORGANIZATIONS; POLICE; INDUSTRIAL FIRST AID; FIRST AID IN THE HOME.

The first aid examination, the prerogative of those great teaching bodies Red Cross and St John, under the searching eye of our honorary treasurer, C.J.M. Adie, burst into life with Edith Winsloe suffering from a nasty cut in the palm of her hand. The examination problems and questions become eloquent, when portrayed in this manner and the make-up and acting of the 'casualty' draws the candidate into the situation and helps to overcome examination nerves. The

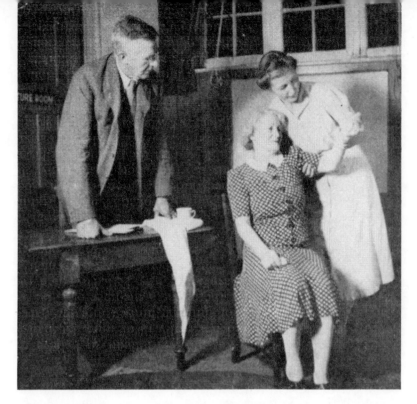

First Aid examination with C.J.M. Adie, and casualty Edith Winsloe

injured person as well as the injury needs to be cared for and prompting is no longer necessary. The need is obvious and follows naturally.

Youth organizations have proved over many years that young people are eager to help others, especially when someone is hurt. They need to be given practical instruction with live but not gruesome illustrations to talks, real 'patients' to bandage, with purpose behind the bandages and situations so they may find out for themselves what has happened. We were happy to receive assistance from Scouts, Guides, and Youth Club members in presenting our case. One November evening Doris Hammer had the writer rescued from a pond on Ranmoor Common by a Rover Scout. He assured us that it was a splendid opportunity. It was cold and the writer was grateful that his prisoner's friend had had the forethought to pack a neat whisky reviver for the corpse from the water. Thanks Doris! It is something I shall never forget.

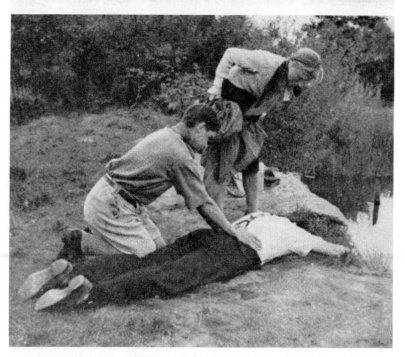

Doris Hammer supervises as Rover Scout gives artificial respiration to the Founder, who had just been pulled out of the water at Frensham Pond

To illustrate what we could do to serve the interests of the police we staged a pedestrian knocked down by a car with policemen doing first aid and controlling the traffic so the situation remained under control in spite of the immediate gathering of a crowd of people both young and old. It is interesting to note Brenda Whiteley rushing out from a house with a blanket, John Loarridge leaning on his bike as part of the crowd, Harry Davies as the distraught driver of the car — nothing was left out. Another offering we made for the police training was Brenda hanging from the rafters of a barn with a rope around her neck looking horribly dead. Police first aid competitions had already claimed our services so we presented such a competition in the brochure. Harry Davies was the 'casualty' having fallen from a high ladder, with John Loarridge as judge making copious notes, and an eager audience amongst whom I can spot George Evershed, Doris Hammer, Brenda Whiteley, John Stevens and the writer.

In industry each section has its own special hazards, particularly in replacing the guards after they have been removed for whatever authorized or unauthorized action. We depict one of our members after a pipe burst in his face while tar-spraying the roads. This is the sort of situation all workers should be prepared to face with appropriate action. We show also Bertie Lowe with his arm trapped in a box-making rolling mill and his damaged arm after his release. One of our members re-enacts an accident that had befallen him previously. The pictures tell their own stories.

The mishaps or accidents that occur in the home are legion and housewives are wise to learn first aid the realistic way. Each exercise that is undertaken is inevitably two faced; it provides opportunity for immediate aid and an urgent reminder of something that should never be allowed to occur again. Our illustrations depict Nancy Budgett caring for Mark Loarridge who had cut his foot on a piece of broken glass. John Stevens had his leg scalded when a disaster occurred with a cracked tea-pot. Brenda Whiteley was in the wars again, when she cut her loaf of bread holding the knife in a dangerous way.

We concluded by a series of excerpts from doctors' letters:-

From Dr. Wm. C. Bentall, O.B.E., F.R.C.S.:

'. . . appreciation of the work which Casualties Union has performed in the war period, and of the value its continuation would confer on all our First-Aid work.'

From Mr W. Rowley Bristow, F.R.C.S.:

'First-Aid work is made infinitely more interesting, and of far greater value, by this realistic represen-tation . . . The enthusiasm shown by the First-Aid workers was obvious, and I am sure that Casualties Union should be called upon to demonstrate to all who are interested in this type of work.'

From Lieutenant-Colonel E.S. Goss, M.C., M.R.C.S., L.R.C.P. (formerly Assistant D.G., E.M.S. Casualty Ser-vices):

'I am convinced that (Casualties Union) will play a large part in future training ... Since the introduction of faked 'casualties' during the war, there is no doubt that a marked improvement has taken place in the handling and treatment of casualties ... this has been largely due to persons carrying out First-Aid having a knowledge of what an injured person looks like, what he feels, and how he will re-act.'

From Dr J.E. Haine, M.B., Ch.B., D.P.H. (Medical Officer of Health):

'I believe that (Casualties Union) has great potentialities, and I look forward to its activities being extended until it is used in all First-Aid or similar training throughout the country. I am sure also that it can be of considerable value in other types of training by providing living examples of the results of accident and disease.'

From Dr E.W. Lowry, M.R.C.S., M.R.C.P., (formerly M.O. B.R.C.S.):

'With my classes, dramatization and demonstration have proved the key to understanding, as opposed to merely attempting to remember ... This method of First-Aid instruction has come to stay ... I feel that the actual teaching of casualty-faking, make-up and acting, should lie outside the training societies, and thus be available to all. To this end, Casualties Union has devoted itself with immense enthusiasm.'

From Mr L.S. Michaelis, M.D., etc., Orthopaedic Surgeon, E.M.S.:

'The most powerful new factor in making instruc-tion live, in preparing the student for the emotional shock, and in bridging the gap between knowledge and experience, has been the work of

Casualties Union ... The sooner it is made available all over the country, entrusted to well-trained instructors, periodically reviewed by the originators, the better.'

From Dr M.M. Pam, M.B., B.S.(Lond).:

'The 'casualty' both helps to teach the student and learns much in the process. The fully-fledged Casualties Union member has to pass tests in the faking of injuries and the representation ... of the part of an injured person: to do this he, or she, must have a sympathetic imagination, and must have realized to an unusual degree the signs, symptoms and appearance of the injury ... This stimulation of sympathetic imagination is of very great value to anyone who aspires to the care of the injured or the training of students.'

From Dr Clive Shields, B.M., B.Ch., M.R.C.S., L.R.C.P.:

'I was fortunate in being able to (receive) help from members of Casualties Union, and I cannot speak too highly of their co-operation ... I feel sure that there is unlimited scope for the activities of the Union in the future in the teaching of First-Aid.'

Whatever the future was to hold for any of us, such confidence in our goodwill and ability from our medical associates and advisers left Casualties Union no alternative than to press on with all the strength it could attract and command.

4

Changes at the Top

Our first president, Mr W.P. Robinson, C.B.E., held on to his responisibilities until the war was over, when he was glad to retire from local government service and felt that he should also stand down as president, now that there was no link remaining with the county council. The union sent a message wishing Mr and Mrs Robinson happiness in their retirement and received this reply: 'Will you kindly convey to the members of the union my heartfelt gratitude for their greetings and good wishes to both of us, and how much pleasure it gives us to learn that the union is not fading away, but its activities are increasing to the benefit of so many.'

We were fortunate to get an introduction to Brigadier W. Rowley Bristow, F.R.C.S., who had served as D.G.M.S. in one of the Mediterranean theatres of war, and he was happy to consider becoming our president. It was a splendid development to have a top level surgeon to lead us into peacetime, setting an example that we have been privileged to maintain.

Shortly after Mr Bristow's appointment, paper rationing controls were lifted, enabling the publication of the first issue of *Casualties Union Journal* and began with:

A MESSAGE FROM THE PRESIDENT
I am writing this short paragraph to wish every success to the first number of the *Casualties Union*

Journal and I hope that, from a small beginning, it will carry on and have a long and prosperous life. The journal will serve a useful purpose in making the work of the union better known, and in stimulating interest for all those who practice first-aid. In this mechanical age their number should indeed be very large with the multiplicity of both road and industrial accidents with which they will be called upon to help.

I have been impressed with the added stimulus that a realistic accident, and a patient, gives to those who are practising or learning first-aid treatment.

I am delighted to have this opportunity of wishing Casualties Union every success in its most useful work.

W. ROWLEY BRISTOW

As we struggled through that winter of 1945/46 we were constantly encouraged by our existing friends. The British Red Cross, St John Ambulance Brigade and the Boy Scouts' Association provided local representatives to speak for them at our council meetings, which was a tremendous help because we were determined to direct our activities into directions that could be of service to each of them. They were Mr A.H.W. Jenkins, Red Cross Assistant County Commissioner for N.E. Surrey; Mr W.G. Pape, O.B.E., St John H.Q. Commissioner and County Commissioner for Surrey; and Mr W.G. Genese, Scout Field Commissioner for Surrey and Middlesex.

We were all very conscious that at that time in particular the medical profession was understaffed and over-burdened, but never failed to give a sympathetic ear to every call, especially from those who were trying to ease the lot of the injured. We needed their advice and guidance to ensure that the right accent was being placed upon the exercises we staged and that the signs we displayed and the symptoms we evinced were correct. It was necessary to woo our potential medical advisers with tact and discretion.

In that first issue of the *Casualties Union Journal* we were able to print articles by Dr J. Edgar Haine, M.B., Ch.B.,

D.P.H. on the future of Casualties Union, and by Mr L.S. Michaelis, M.D. about the make-up and presentation of fractures and associated injuries.

Dr Haine told us that there was no doubt whatever that the quality of training and the standard of first-aid work increased and improved to a remarkable degree as a direct result of the assistance given by Casualties Union. The first-aid personnel were much better fitted psychologically to deal with the real battle casualties. He told us that he had seen that repeatedly, and recalled one rather ghastly incident where the personnel themselves volunteered — and they were most emphatic — that they could never have faced their tasks but for the experience they had had with acting 'casualties'.

He recalled another incident, amusing in retrospect, where a whole exercise had to be cancelled because the ladies of the First-Aid Point, highly efficient and thoroughly trained as they were, were completely knocked off their balance by the reality of our preparations and the realism of the 'casualties', leaving them unable to proceed. He added that it was very quickly apparent that the best first-aid workers in the service were members of Casualties Union. Not that the union had picked the best, he hastened to add, but the training as a 'casualty' gave a better understanding and knowledge, and a more realistic outlook than any form of training previously tried. Of that he stated there is no shadow of doubt.

Dr Haine went on to advise that teaching must become one of our most important functions, the teaching of teachers, so that our principles would be carried far and wide until they reach every first-aid class in the country. As a teaching school or university we should have research in the forefront of our tasks — research into the latest methods and advances. Scientific discoveries should be watched to see what was applicable to our sphere. Again, co-operation with medical science would be all important for the union to advance. Doubtless, too, the union should maintain close co-operation for the union to advance. Doubtless, too, the union should maintain close co-operation with the old established national organizations, but, he warned, keep independent — for independence, coupled with the virility of a youthful organization, would be a great asset, allowing the union to strike out in new directions.

Finally he told us that Casualties Union was one of the really important and worthwhile things to have emerged from the war. That experience must never be lost. It was, he believed, only in its infancy but he suggested was no longer local or even county in character. Call it national, or call it universal. It is of universal application. He warned us to preserve our enthusiasm, our high traditions of service, to prepare our organization to meet with every development and he concluded that he had no doubts the union would take its rightful place in the scheme of things, and blaze a trail which all would regard with justifiable pride.

As one thinks back on this advice one hopes that the late Dr Haine would feel that we had in some measure lived up to his expectations.

Other experts generously contributed their experiences to help us to complete a picture of the scope of service we were undertaking. W. Whitbourn, St.J.A.B., Superintendent, Guildford Baths, gave 'Some Notes on Asphyxia'.

5

Widening the Circle of Action

On two successive weekends in December 1945, demonstrations were mounted in Croydon at the request of the Red Cross and in January 1946, we were able to hold a similar course at Reading at the behest of St John. Here we met H.F. Skidmore and one of the junior members — a very young John Wise. As a result of these courses we were able to build up branches in Croydon, Wallington and Reading. 'Skiddy', as H.F. Skidmore was known to his friends, was a long experienced driver of mainline steam trains and was able to lead Casualties Union into the railway world. A further demonstration was given in Croydon in February for members St John Ambulance Brigade in South London.

Another outlet was offered to the union by a liaison John Stevens developed with *The Nursing Mirror*. The union co-operated in producing photographs to illustrate articles on Industrial First-Aid, which they were about to publish. The incidents portrayed took place against authentic backgrounds; a laboratory, a corn store, a railway siding, a boiler room and at a turret lathe in an engineering workshop. The acknowledgements accompanying these illustrated articles introduced Casualties Union to a wide public who had never heard of the union or its services previously.

The Nursing Mirror permitted us to reproduce an article by Mr Harold Burrows, C.B.E., Ph.D., F.R.C.S. on 'Nervous Reactions to Physical Emergencies,' discussing fear, pain and muscular weakness. This was useful in giving a finer edge to our responsive acting. 'Sudden dangers,' he concluded, 'if they do not lead to panic, are usually unaccompanied by fear. Sudden severe injuries do not cause pain at the time of infliction. Muscular weakness, which may be general, is a common transitory effect of wounds.'

Dr A.L. Fraser gave us an article on 'Haemorrhage,' carrying our education still further and we studied 'Children in Road Accidents' with the Royal Society for the Prevention of Accidents. We learnt that in 1945 nearly one quarter of all fatal casualties were children, two thirds of whom were under seven years of age.

Were I to state that we held the fourth annual general meeting — the first postwar — at Eton College, I should mislead my readers, but it was held on Fellow's Eyot, a riverside part of the college grounds, when our guest of honour was none other than Sir Henry Marten, the Provost of Eton College. We had been granted permission to erect marquees, tents, hoardings mounted with large photographs, car parks and arenas marked off by rope barriers and of course there was a public address van.

Members had all come in mufti as if to emphasise their total independence of all other organizations. Among the crowd that thronged the meadows were many uniforms of Red Cross and St John nurses and men, Rovers, Rangers, Scouts and Guides, to say nothing of the many scholars in their black suits and 'toppers' from Eton College itself.

Lunch for visitors gave an opportunity for Casualties Union to hold its AGM and then at their lunch to find themselves welcomed by Charley Smallbone — remembered by most people as 'Sambo' from the wartime rescue school — a happy occasion.

Sir Henry Marten, Provost of Eton College, himself welcomed us to the college and the President of Casualties Union, Brigadier Rowley Bristow, replied in suitable terms stressing the advances that the union had made in the teaching and learning of First-Aid compared with earlier days when as a regimental M.O. he had tied labels onto volunteers in order to give some practice for stretcher bearers.

The honorary organizer, returning thanks to the two

speakers, emphasised that 'service' was a message for peace. It was one of the great traditions of Eton and other fine schools. If true service involved the abandonment of orthodoxy, let them be unorthodox as long as they knew in their hearts that they were doing the right thing. In the union their was room for every profession every type of person, and work waiting for them. Enquiries for Casualties Union training were coming in from all over the British Isles and from the Dominions. Real service was needed in a practical way if the union was to provide all the facilities for which it was asked.

Then followed a Diagnosis Competition under the direction of Miss Doris Hammer. This was an eye-opener for almost everyone, because practise in diagnosis had never been possible before the development of Casualties Union technique. The competition was won by The British Red Cross, Surrey Esher Division Ladies.

A rescue contest under the direction of Roy Stokes, B.E.M., was also staged with a 'casualty' caught in the V between two sloping sections of timber. The 'casualty' was suffering from injuries both to her head and one leg. Each team carried out the extrication and treatment, watched closely by two doctors. We felt that apart from the interest such a situation would create, the V was a suitable sign for the victories the Allies had so recently earned at so great a price. St John Ambulance Brigade, South Bucks Corps, were the winners.

The day was a great success; the complex organization had worked with hardly a single hitch. However, at the end of a happy day came the clearing up! What a team everything was soon stored away without too much strain. From what fine stuff Casualties Union members are made! When all was over perhaps one had hoped for some constructive publicity — the *Daily Mirror* reported the reunion at Eton under the headline, THEY LAUGHED TO SEE SUCH AGONY. While acknowledging gratefully this notice being taken of our activities the editor of the journal felt bound to 'correct our august contemporary on a matter of fact. Our visitors were more in earnest than it evidently imagines: there were serious and interested enquiries. However we will permit ourselves a smile — and no more — over the queer tricks that popular journalism must play. Essentially, Casualties Union is not a stunt — it means business.'

Of course we needed also to build up our knowledge and technique if we were to attract a wider public. Dr Milicent Pam gave us a splendid article on 'Injuries to the Head', which gave us a wide range of possiblities both with and without visible or concealed injuries.

At the same time *The Practitioner* courteously allowed us to reproduce excerpts from 'Modern Views on Concussion' by Dr Fergus R. Ferguson, M.D., F.R.C.P., D.P.H. and Dr L.A. Liversedge, B.Sc., M.B., Ch.B. of the Neurological Department of the University of Manchester and Manchester Royal Infirmary.

All the while we were building up our technical understanding and we needed also to ensure that we kept our ideas directed towards accident causation during those times, so that our energies might be schemed in both topical and typical directions if our realism was to help others. One of our members Barry Robinson of the Surrey County Ambulance Service contributed information on 'Domestic Accidents' telling who was affected, where in the house or garden and how they changed with age from toddlers to senile octogenarians. They included tumbles, burns, scalds, smashes as with sash windows with broken cords, tripping and falling onto sharp objects, poisoning, diabetic coma, electric shock and a hundred more to stir the imagination of Casualties Union members and hopefully provide provocative training by Red Cross, St John, Scouts, Guides, Railway staff, Police, Territorial Army and others.

A timely warning came from John Loarridge, one of the senior instructors, who had been visiting branches, that there was danger in the quality of union work being ruined by undue haste due to lack of time being provided. Make-up was suffering badly and, to a slightly less degree, so was staging. Make-up must harmonise with the staging and vice versa. Also behaviour must be carefully considered and controlled to be appropriate to the make-up and the staging. An 'accident' must always be consistent.

6

Make-up

Throughout this critical period make-up was much under review. False tissue was difficult. Putty which had been valuable during the war, gradually deteriorated as it became blended with fish oil in place of linseed oil, then in short supply, and was less manageable. Plasticine began to take its place but unlike putty it was difficult to blend colours to a satisfactory shade to match the varying shades of one person's skin, let alone provide for universal skin colourings.

The research sub-committee under Mrs Brenda Whiteley picked up all the suggestions made by members as well as those devised by the members of her group. Cold cream putty could be made by mixing whiting into cold cream. The use of vaseline somewhat generously to merge the edges of false tissue into the adjoining flesh was easily dried off by powdering with two coats of magnesium powder.

Mr Alex Garden, a research chemist and one of our supporter members, gave us a formula for making artificial flesh from which to make artificial limbs — somewhat cheaper than the dental jelly used for making moulds of the mouth, when preparing artificial teeth which Cortazzi had used during the war. The latter looked well and felt well but lacked the strength to withstand the knocking about inseparable from handling in rescue situations. The materials and method were:

Gelatine Powder	3	lbs.
Water	4½	lbs.
Glycerine	7½	lbs.
Keiselguhr	1½	lbs.
Solution of Aramanth Dye	½	fl.oz.

'Pour all the water rapidly onto the gelatine powder and stir quickly and thoroughly, so that all the powder is wetted with the water. Allow the gelatine water mixture to stand about 30 minutes in order that the gelatine may swell and take up the water and then melt the mixture in a boiling water bath. When the gelatine has gone completely into solution, add the glycerine, mix well and then add the kieselguhr, taking care to rub out any lumpy pieces with the stirrer. Finally add the colour solution and stir well. Remove the vessel from the water bath and set aside for ten minutes to allow the scum to rise to the surface. This scum is removed with a large spoon and discarded. The mixture can now be cast into oiled trays and allowed to set, when it may be cut into suitable sized pieces and stored in a cool place.

'When making a casting it is only necessary to take a suitable quantity of the material and melt in an earthenware pot in a boiling water bath. The temperature should be about 50 degrees C., not higher, when the casting is made. Prolonged heating should be avoided. Large castings, such as arms, legs, etc., have to be reinforced with suitably shaped pieces of bone, wood or wire (cf. Cortazzi's method). The mould is better made of Plaster of Paris, and the surface should be coated with vaseline. The best method is to melt the vaseline and to paint it onto the plaster surface with a brush. Two coats of the above should be given on successive days, as the first coat is largely absorbed by the plaster. Be careful to avoid leaving blobs of vaseline on any part of the casting, otherwise the fine markings (such as the lines of the skin) are not produced in the 'flesh'. Leave the 'flesh' at least one day in the mould before turning out, which has to be very carefully done. The 'flesh' casting may, of course, be made-up by the usual faking procedure with greasepaints, etc., but first of all dry the surface with a trace of powdered chalk or talc so that the paint will adhere. Regarding the supply of the materials, you may find it difficult at the present time to obtain the powdered gelatine, which must be of high grade, but you might try your local pharmacist, who may be able to get it for you. The other materials should be stocked by large pharmacies. The above recipe should make about sixteen pounds of 'flesh'.'

At this time we had started using collodion to incorporate skin markings on well blended plasticine. Flesh, stone, white, yellow and terracotta were in the proportions 5:5:3:1:1. The problem with all false tissues is that they tend, when well blended, to have a uniform colour, whereas the natural flesh colouring as seen through the human skin is mottled. So the coating of the area with collodion helped the vein lines painted in to be set and a slight mottling to be applied with the finger tips and permit any hair to be replaced, where false tissue had covered hirsute areas. The advantages claimed were that such injuries could be swabbed and dressed during normal procedures used in First-Aid stations.

Members, both new and not so new, proved to be most ingenious in creating bloods to be incorporated in different situations — to flow freely, to coagulate, to ooze, and so on — using sugar and artists' colours. 'Blood' for use in severe bleeding from arteries or major veins had of course to be free from any thickening to allow it to be forced through small tubes within the make-up.

So make-up techniques began to develop beyond the limits possible during wartime.

7

Expansion

By mid-summer 1946 requests for training began to be received from distant parts of our own country and overseas. There was no way we could provide direct tuition at home in the limited time at our disposal, let alone overseas, where interest was being shown in Israel, South Africa and New Zealand. So we decided on a bold experiment of correspondence courses. We set up a system of study groups under leaders who could inspire their fellow members to transend all difficulties and follow the written guidance, which was supported by advice from one of our experts, which could be enlisted through correspondence until the difficulty was overcome.

In this way the Study Circle Scheme was launched before the autumn of 1946. It was necessary for potential members to be guided to cover the full training and not merely to dabble in make-up, which appeared to be the major attraction. Even today it has to be the least of Casualties Union's arts, which we listed in order of importance as acting, staging, planning, make-up. In spite of the obvious truth in the above statement, make-up has a dominant attraction for some members with the risk that they are neglecting the other three.

One thing is certain, when make-up is necessary, it must be discrete and quite perfect so as to be obviously real. Second class make-up always betrays an otherwise excellent 'casualty' portrayal.

Not surprisingly some of the interested parties soon lost their enthusiasm when they discovered that they had to work hard if they were to master the full technique and pass the tests to become members of Casualties Union. Most of them were first aiders or nurses, so they had some knowledge of the human body and how it behaves but the Study Circle training is a challenging course.

Those who opted out often did not wish to pay and with the union's meagre financial resources in those days make-up materials were difficult to obtain except in expensive packs. To help students to get started the union issued sample packs as part of the Study Circle equipment. These were enough to carry them through the initial training. Instead of providing sticks of grease paint, a Study Circle was provided with crown cork bottle caps, each filled with a colour. Likewise all the materials provided were limited to the estimated amount the circle would need. It is well to learn at the outset that the less make-up used, the less false tissue used, the more natural the 'casualty' appears to be.

However it was also necessary to impress upon would-be members that many casualties do not experience visible bleeding, or discolouring or deformity, so that the whole situation is expressed in the acting of the casualty. The behaviour, the answers to questions and the responses to the things going on around one and the reaction to handling and treatment or neglect that the casualty experiences.

Study Circle number one was at Cottingham, Hull, under the leadership of Miss E.H. Browne, a St John Officer. It started in autumn 1946. The circle was entirely successful and Miss Browne went on eagerly to part three of the Study Circle notes and became an instructor. This enabled Cottingham Study Circle to become a branch in July, 1947. It is leadership and drive that ensures success.

Amongst the first dozen circles launched before the end of 1947 were Vauxhall, Luton; Cambridge; Haifa, Palestine; Sutton, Surrey; Rhondda, South Wales; Cape Town, South Africa; Dublin; and Romford, Essex. Most of them struggled for two or three years before giving up, but Cambridge, Rhondda, Romford and Cape Town were successful. This seemed to confirm the value of the Study Circle system of instruction and it is interesting to note that Cape Town's success led to the formation of many more circles, all under the influence of the same dynamic man, R.J. Nicoll, who had reached out to Casualties Union through Scouting, and who undertook to be branch organizer for the Dominion of South Africa.

A valuable piece of publicity came in the 21st December, 1946, issue of *The Lancet* and the editor kindly gave the union permission to reproduce it.

BATTLE SCHOOL FOR FIRST AIDERS

Plainly, it is impossible to teach first aid workers the theory behind all that they learn. This being so, instruction tends to take the form of rigid dogma, teachers and pupils counting themselves content if the catechism is accurately remembered; and the same is true of the usual formal exercises. Top marks in a test under these conditions is no guarantee of even a passable showing in the rough and tumble of reality. This consideration prompted the founding of Casualties Union, which is dedicated to realism in training. The Union teaches the first aider to use his intelligence as well as his memory; the training he is offered is based on war-time experience that he can no more identify and treat by the 1, 2, 3 in the little book than can the doctor recognize and relieve the condition of his patients by recall of the classical description in the textbook. The Union has been at pains to train actors in the role of 'casualties', and to make them look the part; the autumn number of the Union's journal, for example contains articles on faking of flesh wounds and a formula for washable blood. It only remains for the casualty to be found in a realistic environment — on the road, pinned under a beam, or in a smoke filled room — and the stage is set for a first-class exercise. The aims of the union, whose branches are multiplying in the home counties, will be applauded by all those who are interested in better first aid.

It is hardly necessary to mention what a boost this gave to the morale of the founder members. It is not possible to say how much influence this article had upon the medical profession; all one can say is that we have always received supportive assistance from our medical friends everywhere. We hope and believe we have not betrayed their trust, nor shall we, so long as we maintain our own high standard of total realism.

Indeed we continued to be provided with articles to guide our progress. Dr Thomas Yoxall wrote about 'Abdominal Injuries'; Mr L.S. Michaelis presented us with 'Injuries to the Spine'; Dr L.A. Eastwood added 'Burns and Scalds — their Signs and Symptoms'; while Dr J.E. Haine advised upon the care needed in 'The Use of Atropine for Casualties Union Work'. Dr R.B. McMillan taught us about 'Types of Insensibility', and Dr R.E.J. Kerr helped us over 'The Breathing of Casualties'.

All this help reached us, much of it from outside sources during the first three years of peace and as the years passed, they never failed us.

8

New Types of Competition

It was felt that competitions with total realism which had been developed during the war with the aid of members of Casualties Union should be available to all groups of enthusiastic first aiders. We had given some hints to the public at Eton, but these had all come to take part by invitation. Could we stage realistic events in which first aid teams would request to compete?

One of our senior instructors Harry Davies, who had been leader of a rescue party during the war, was an expert mechanic for London Transport at the Chiswick Road Transport Depot, Chiswick, London, and by his good offices we were invited to hold our fifth annual reunion there in June, 1947. We advertised the main open competitions for silver challenge trophies, one for diagnosis and the other for first aid. These had been made available to me by an old friend, C.R.B. Tingey, a specialist in trophy sculpting, of John Bull, County Gold & Silversmiths, High Street, Bedford. He created for us two reproductions in pure silver of the old-fashioned bleeding bowls used with leeches by physicians of old.

I was able to persuade Mr John A. Tulk, chairman of the Surrey County Council, under whose jurisdiction Casualties Union had been formed, to present one of the bowls, to be held for one year by the team doing best in first aid. The president and officers of the union kindly donated the other bowl to be held for one year by the team best in the diagnosis contest. They were duly returned to the silversmith for appropriate engraving and return in time for the great day. They were returned by registered post but got caught up in a mail jam at King's Cross, caused by industrial action, and nothing could budge the authorities to release the package.

Bertie Lowe was chairman of the reunion committee and took everything in his stride. There were lots of teams so he had the problem repeated some six times and the "casualties" and the judges were briefed to behave in identical ways so that the best overall team could be chosen in a short time. Each "casualty was trapped by the wrist under a bicycle wheel, itself crushed by the wheel of a car. Roy Stokes made a splendid job of this production line.

Similarly Doris Hammer produced ring after ring of casualties for all the participants in the diagnosis arena. Both magnificently identified their winners. The day ended with two damaged buses being staged together as if their damaged areas had been caused by a collision between them. All the members of Casualties Union crammed into the buses as "casualties" and the united force of first aiders on parade had a field day in rescuing them.

Finally the dread moment came for the presentation of the trophies, which I had to admit had got held up in the post on the railway. We therefore arranged to have a ceremonial presentation on the following Sunday outside the union's official address John Loarridge's offices in Bedford Row, London. This was recorded by Sidney Francis with his camera and duly publicized.

Bertie Lowe paid tribute afterwards — 'As chairman of the reunion committee, I should like to take this opportunity of thanking all members who turned up on June 22 for the excellent support given by them to the producers of the competitions for first aid and diagnosis, and of the mass incident that followed. There in no doubt that from the competitors' and visitors' point of view the day's proceedings were an outstanding success.

'I took the opportunity of speaking to many of the competitors and guests, and am pleased to state that your efforts called forth universal praise. The reactions of many of the teams in the competitions were interesting — the

The belated presentation by Brenda Whiteley to the
Red Cross winners of the Reproduction Bleeding
Bowl for Diagnosis competition

following is the kind of comment frequently made:

> "We were certainly surprised by the thoroughness
> of the test; we know that we dropped marks and
> made mistakes. We do not expect to win but we
> have thoroughly enjoyed the opportunity of hand-
> ling a realistic and live situation. This is how we
> should like all competitions to be staged, and we
> look forward to competing on future occasions."

'This, of course, proves that you succeeded in putting
over the union technique in a most convincing manner. The
result will be shown in the number of entries for next year's
competitions. It is confidently anticipated that the entries
will be so large that eliminating tests will have to be run off
on dates prior to the reunion. This will mean further calls
upon your services; that these will be answered with your
usual enthusiasm I have no doubt.

'In closing, I would like to thank particularly all those
non-members who so kindly assisted us at Chiswick.'

In the following year, 1948, for our sixth annual reunion

A Red Cross team in action at Nine Elms depot
Photo by courtesy of The Studio, Barons Court Station

we were the guests of British Railways at the Southern Region Goods Depot at Nine Elms, Vauxhall, London. The diagnosis 'casualties' were all staged on the railway track amongst goods wagons. The first aid problem consisted of a mechanic who had been caught under the rear axle of a mechanical horse tractor which had been driven away inadvertently by a driver who failed to notice the mechanic working underneath. Fifty-six teams competed including a women's team and we were indebted to Roy Stokes and Doris Hammer for devising and staging these competitions with most willing assistance from the railway staff.

During the interval, while the scrutineers were making up the final scores, Brenda Whiteley, Harry Davies and Bertie Lowe gave a demonstration showing how acting, staging, planning and make-up combined to make a 'casualty' for first aid training, and Bertie Lowe explained why the union refused to encourage make-up on its own.

Dr H.C. Lang, the deputy chief staff officer of the British Railways Southern Region presented the trophies and chatted to each of the members of the winning teams and the runners up.

The Territorial Army was our host in 1949 at its headquarters at The Duke of York's Barracks at South Kensington, for our seventh annual reunion. Our guest of honour was Wing Commander Sir John Hodsoll, C.B., and appropriate to his Air Force connection, we staged our first aid contest on the theme of a parachutist who had landed badly and in some trouble with his 'chute.

9

A Message from the Home Office

Sir John Hodsoll had been a great supporter of Casualties Union since its inception and had found its services advantageous wherever he had encountered it. He continued to support us in his capacity of vice-president after the stand down of Civil Defence and no doubt he, perhaps more than most people, was in a position to know about the dangers ahead and the need for readiness. He wrote a communique to the union:

> 'It will not, I hope, be very long now before Civil Defence is again restored to the map. It comes back to take its place as an essential and integral part of the permanent defence system of the country. It is important to emphasise this point. Developments in weapons and tactics have made it just as important to have a sound Civil Defence organization as it is to have an efficient active defence. The two together make up the balanced pattern of Home Defence on which so much of the security of this country depends.
>
> 'The new service will have some formidable technical and tactical problems to face, and they can only be overcome by the keenness and enthusiasm of the volunteers, backed up by sound knowledge and appreciation of the problems and by undergoing the most up-to-date training.

Civil Defence in action once more, the casualty is Alwyn Law

Photo by courtesy of Isle of Thanet Gazette

'I have followed with the greatest interest and pleasure the successful work of Casualties Union since the war. There in no doubt in my mind that the development of what I think can rightly be termed the science of producing realistic casualties, is making a big and important contribution to the training and the skill of all those who will have first-aid duties to carry out, not only in war time but also in peace. Once training starts, first-aid will play an important part, and it is my hope and desire to get as many people as possible to take some first-aid training, quite apart from those who will be especially concerned with this branch of the service. The new weapons, such as the atomic bomb and the new types of gas, will all produce new first-aid problems. To some of them we have as yet no answer, but I feel certain that continued scientific study, combined with practical experiment, will gradually enable us to master these problems, at any rate to a very considerable extent. The production of realistic casualties to

54

simulate those who might have been affected by the new weapons will obviously be a most important part of future training. I look forward to the very closest co-operation with Casualties Union, remembering as I do so well the magnificent contribution they made during the war. I am very anxious that their technique and all their experience should be available in the widest possible field, and I feel sure that it will be possible to effect this close co-operation to the great benefit of the future efficiency of Civil Defence.'

In these early post war years we proceeded from one challenge to another and I hope and believe we were able to fulfill every one and satisfy everyone who looked to us for inspiration as well as skilled assistance of a high standard.

10

The Buxton Trophy

We were fortunate in 1950 for our eighth annual reunion to be guests of the proprietors of Hay's Wharf Limited who put the waterfront and the yards behind at our disposal. It was an admirable site giving interesting backgrounds to a variety of accident situations.

The Buxton Trophy, generously presented to the union by our president, Brigadier St John Buxton, M.B., B.S., F.R.C.S., the master trophy for first-aid plus diagnosis contests, was competed for the very first time in 1950, and took place on the quayside amongst the towering cranes. It is held for one year by the team gaining highest aggregate marks in first-aid and diagnosis.

A large scale demonstration was also staged so that spectators who had seen one or two teams compete could then direct their attention to the ways in which the union technique was being used to assist the first-aid societies with their training programmes. In one part, dock life went on as usual with the miscellaneous accidents occurring at a rather greater frequency than usual. This was arranged to show the rather large variety of cases for which there can be no make-up since there is no deformity, discolouration or disfigurement that can be shown by plastic or greasepaint. It is the circumstances and behaviour alone in these cases from which diagnosis can be made, and staging and acting only are required to depict them.

Elsewhere, a parachutist, who had baled out over the

Nellie Sand has hysteria at the docks

docks, struck his head on one of the buildings, got his parachute caught on one of the cranes, and broken his leg in the lines of the parachute. Another accident showed a docker struck by falling sacks which had knocked him down, burst and smothered him.

The shielding power of buildings and of different materials was indicated by a representation of a building partially affected by radiation from an atomic bomb burst two miles away. A woman working on the roof suffered from flashburn.

Another item showed many dozens of things which might cause wounds. They ranged from the scythe of the farmer to the butcher' chopper, and from the housewife's needle to the hammer and clink of the roadside navvy. These suggest the wide scope for variation in both site of accident and severity of injury so that there need be no departure from the realistic setting in staging accidents for first-aid training or for competitions.

The trophies were presented by Lieutenant-Colonel E.S. Goss, M.C., well known to many as Assistant Director of Medical Services and an honorary member of the union. He cited the aims of the union and paid tribute to the work which it was doing.

Dame Beryl Oliver, British Red Cross Society's Director of Education, writing afterwards, summed up the proceedings in this way: 'I should like to thank Casualties Union most warmly for the interesting afternoon I spent with you all yesterday. Enormous trouble had been taken to make the afternoon such a successful one, and the various competitions cannot fail to have been most instructive to all concerned. The setting of the competition at Hay's Wharf was particularly unusual and valuable as it gave the opportunity of seeing accidents handled in their appropriate surroundings.'

For our ninth annual reunion, in 1951, Casualties Union was once again guests of British Railways, at King's Cross Station, where platforms 16 and 17 had been placed at our disposal. As before we were already amongst friends but particularly with Dr John Binning, Pat Stokoe and the members of Study Circle No 152. As always it was an inspiring event and tremedously enjoyed by competitors and spectators alike.

I I

Tenth Annual Reunion

Messrs Terson's Limited, the building firm, were our hosts for the 1952 competitions and they managed to provide us a very different and challenging site to stage our competitions. They were in process of building a block of flats in Holford Square, Finsbury, London.

Thirty-two teams took part. They came from all over the country and included teams from the T.A., R.A.M.C., from various departments of industry, from three pits of the National Coal Board, and from a variety of divisions and detachments of St John Ambulance Brigade and British Red Cross Society. All teams competed in a first-aid team test and an individual test in diagnosis. Each team was presented with an identical set, complete with ladders reaching from the ground to the fifth storey, and the first aiders were called upon to deal with three casualties in each set.

Berkshire 74 (Nursing Division) S.J.A.B. from Maidenhead won the Buxton Trophy and the Trophy for First Aid; Kent 99 British Red Cross Society were successful in winning the Diagnosis Trophy for the second year running.

Mr James Paterson, M.C., chairman of the board of Messrs Tersons, and Mrs Paterson, were guests of honour, and presented the trophies to the winning teams. Side-shows were provided by the Institute of Civil Defence and the Royal Society for the Prevention of Accidents, and an information centre was manned by Casualties Union. In

59

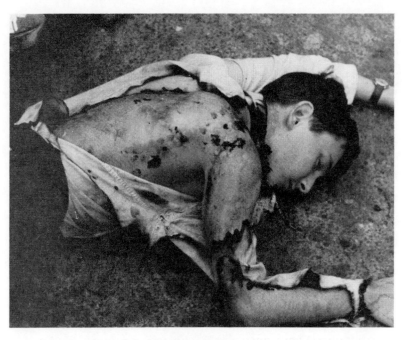

A garage hand who was smoking too close to petrol fumes.
Casualty is Arthur Smith

addition there was a special meeting place for members of
Study Circles, where senior instructors answered questions
and gave demonstrations on make-up and staging. Instruction on the Holger Neilson method of artificial resperation
drew big crowds throughout the afternoon.

An impressive demonstration was provided by the
R.A.M.C. Visual Aid Team from Queen Elizabeth Barracks,
Crookham, Hampshire, showing battle casualties. This
demonstration called forth special comment from many
visitors including doctors.

12

Changing the Scene

At the start of 1949 a valuable contribution to realism in competition work was sponsored by the Editor of *First Aid and Nursing* in the form of a conference of all interested bodies. It was encouraging to find the importance already attached to realism in setting competition tests. While there were diverse views on detail, there was unaminity regarding realism in principle. I would like to record my great appreciation, I wrote at that time, of the initiative of Mr Dale Smith in promoting such a conference and to congratulate Dr G.O. Hughes who took the chair and Mr F.C. Trott who was responsible for preparing the agenda. It was a first step, but a positive step, towards better first aid.

In 1949 Casualties Union was again invited, through John Loarridge, to assist with the final rounds of the Stanley Shield Competitions and the British Red Cross Society made some slight amendments to their rules:

> Competitors must be prepared to deal with 'casualties' whose injuries have been faked, and to recognize the signs and symptoms portrayed by casualty-faking and the acting of the 'patients'.
>
> It must be borne in mind that the judge is closely observing their work, and it is therefore unneccessary for competitors to explain what is being done, but essential questions relative to the condition of the patient, may be asked both of the

patient and the judge.

The union was invited during this year, in many of the eliminating rounds as well as the final, to take part in the planning and producing of the problems as well as the staging of the incidents. The final of the Stanley Shield was an impressive occasion. Both men's and women's competitions proceeded simultaneously and the Princess Royal, the Commander-in-Chief of the Red Cross Society, presided. Her Royal Highness took the greatest interest in the staging of both competitions and presented the trophies to the winners. The winner of the Women's Trophy was the Red Cross team from Ilfracombe, who had been studying the union technique through Study Circle No. 33 at Ilfracombe. The individual who gained the highest number of marks in the competition was Miss Berry, the Study Circle secretary. The problem was good but there were difficulties in staging to satisfy both the needs of the spectators and the competitors. The acting of the casualties was satisfactory, but while their performance was convincing enough, they appeared to be tied to a pattern of response that was rather too rigid to be realistic.

In *Red Cross Quarterly Review* for July, 1949, the following comment was made regarding the Stanley Shield Competitions — 'A word must be said about the long suffering 'casualties'. Members of Casualties Union gave themselves unsparingly throughout the day and their work was exacting. It is no easy task to throw a realistic epileptic fit over and over again, or to be overcome by coal gas several times during the day. So much of the realism of the tests depends upon the convincing acting of the 'casualties', and a special vote of thanks should go to these people who did their work so well.'

13

British Red Cross Society National Training Centre

The society invited the union to mount a weekend course at their National Training Centre at the beginning of July 1949 for potential leaders of Study Circles. Miss Monica Bond, the Commandant of Barnett Hill, at Wonersh, in Surrey, made everyone very welcome. There were some forty students and five senior instructors belonging to the union. At intervals during the weekend some of our Surrey members came in out of the blue having had an accident. It was a hectic course for both students and instructors, but most rewarding.

One of the students, Dr Isabelle W. Horsley, M.B., Ch.B., (County Director B.R.C.S., Cornwall), made the following comments:

'We all regretted when the course came to an end; we realized we had learnt a tremendous amount in a short time, and the teaching was so clever that seldom were we told or shown what to do; we were shown how to use our brains and produce the necessary results ourselves.

'The members of Casualties Union have brought this new method to a very high art and, as they say, their work is revolutionary, and in the future our first-aid classes will consist of treating these very accurate casualties, instead of simply tying each other up in triangular bandages. By this new method one will be much more ready to treat the real thing when one meets it. Also by learning to act the part one has to know the signs and symptoms very thoroughly, otherwise the acting would not be correct.

'Everyone pronounced this weekend a huge success and we are very grateful to the Casualties Union members for all they gave us from Friday night to Monday morning . . . we were . . . ready waiting . . . on our return . . . to set up our own Study Circles and try to qualify to become members of this Casualties Union.'

Suddenly there was a great demand for demonstrations of union technique to be presented locally for the countrywide membership of B.R.C.S. and senior instructors were scurrying here and there with parties of demonstrators. Not surprisingly after the comments of Dr Isabelle Horsley, we had been to Truro in Cornwall on 14 May, just one week after the Red Cross Stanley Shield competitions. A fortnight later we were off to Cambridge on the Saturday and onto Norwich for the Sunday. Then to Southampton in Hampshire and two months later we were back again at Winchester. In the meantime we had been to Brighton in Sussex and to Grantham in South Lincolnshire; to Bristol in Somerset; and to Leeds in Yorkshire; to Birmingham in Warwickshire; to Scotland several times in Glasgow and also on another trip to Edinburgh and later to Aberdeen. In between we went to Brighton again and honoured a request to visit Andover in Hampshire.

The demand for courses at Barnett Hill was greatly stimulated by these visits and the interest that spread over each area as a result. A second course was held in 1949 and at least one course has been run every year since for some forty would-be leaders of Study Circles.

On average some twenty Circles have been founded each year through the decades that have passed since then. Not all of them owed alliegence to Red Cross, but creating a corps of skilled 'casualties' upon whom the society could call.

14

Into Scotland

This was held on the weekend of 22 and 23 October, 1949 at Red Cross Headquarters, Bath Street, Glasgow. Fifty-four members of the Scottish Red Cross took part in the course. The welcome received from the moment of arrival is something that has long remained in the memories of the eight members of the union who had travelled overnight from the South of England. Over sixty different 'casualties' were presented and nine fully staged 'accidents' were produced.

The first session contrasted past, present and suggested future training methods. The present method of adopting realistic practices when trained 'patients' are available was represented by an amatueur electrician splicing a temporary lamp for the lecture table on to a flex carrying an electric fire. When the current was switched on there was a small flash and the electrician was flung across the room, his lighted cigarette falling to the floor, and there he lay inert and unbreathing with his left hand in spasm still clutching the flex, which was seen to be still alive because the fire was alight. Momentarily the startled audience sat spellbound; then someone picked up the cigarette, someone else righted the fire that had fallen over, a third switched off the power, and a fourth set about giving artificial respiration. When at last the hand was freed from the cable, it was found to be deeply burned, with charred flesh and blistering. This was agreed to be first-class training, but at that time only available 'when you could get it.'

Possibilities for the future were illustrated by a 'cavalcade' of 'casualties' presented to the audience as a bandage practice. For an hour they came in at intervals of a few minutes until the whole of the course in parties of four had each handled a 'casualty'.

A welcome pause for tea followed but for the 'casualties' it meant fresh preparations for the diagnosis exercises which followed. Three series of six cases were staged and one-third of the audience diagnosed each of the six cases while the other two-thirds watched in well-disciplined silence. The various cases:

Series 1	Series 2	Series 3
Compression.	Sprained ankle.	Fractured base.
Concussion.	Bruised shin.	Faint with recovery.
Asphyxia with sawdust.	Fractured ribs.	Internal haemmorhage.
Sleep.	Punctured lungs (gun-	Fractured Pelvis.
Alcoholic poisoning.	shot entry wound	Fractured Spine.
Diabetic coma.	only).	Concussion with open tibia.

The first day ended with a short display of make-up and acting in which the audience in four groups each saw a 'casualty' made-up, briefed and rehearsed and then saw the completed make-up and acting of the other three 'patients'.

The second day began with a street accident on Bath Street outside Red Cross Headquarters involving a car and a bicycle. The Glasgow City Police appeared upon the scene and took charge of the situation, passing the bus traffic through with absolute calm. A Red Cross First-Aid party attended to the 'patients', who were taken to hospital in an ambulance provided and manned by St Andrew. The climax was provided by St Andrew dispatching a second ambulance, and the bus service sending their breakdown service. They 'knew that it was a real accident' because:

- the skidmarks on the road and the mud under the wings showed how violently the car had stopped;
- money and other oddments were scattered over the street from the cyclist's handbag.

Six further accidents were then staged inside the building. These were each staged four times. The course was split into

A training course at Glasgow with Mrs Douglas Johnston

six groups; each group dealt with three of the situations and had an opportunity of seeing the problem provided in the staging of the other three situations. Reconstruction of the flue for the oil-fired central heating boiler, which was only partially completed, gave opportunity for some interesting situations with a variety of injuries.

The afternoon session set out to show how the eight-lecture Red Cross Course and Bandage practices could be illustrated by the union technique. The following cases were shown:

- Unconscious (concussion) recovering, bleeding from hand, broken collar bone.
- Dislocated shoulder.
- Sprained wrist.
- Closed fracture of tibia becoming open.
- Broken neck of femur.
- Fractured patella.
- Crushed foot in shoe.

67

- Internal haemmorhage, abdomen.
- Severed arm (shoulder).
- Varicose veins.
- Various degrees of burns.
- Smashed face.
- Shock (delayed).
- Eye transfixed with fragment of glass.
- Epilepsy.
- Coal gas asphyxia.
- Drowning.

During a pause in this sequence, the union wartime film was shown and the Study Circles' training scheme was described. Colonel Arthur, the secretary of the Scottish branch of the British Red Cross Society, paid a warm tribute to the union's methods and asked that Study Circles be formed throughout the area. This was a milestone, perhaps, in our development north of the border.

15

Headquarters News

Meeting at headquarters: Left to right, Eric Claxton,
Johnnie Johnson, Winnie Elston, Joan Brackin,
Pitts, Mary Murphy, Lance Wills, Cyril Wallis

Official decisions continued to guide us. Mrs E.L. (Steve)
Eaton of Reading branch was appointed a senior instructor.
An executive sub-committee was appointed on 13 November,
1949, which was to meet fortnightly in London with power
to authorize the officers of the union to act. It was
answerable for its decisions to the full committee, which
continued to meet quarterly as before. The members first
appointed to the Executive Sub-Committee were myself and
messrs Davies, Loarridge, Pitts, Sargeant, Stevens and
Towndrow and Miss Crockford. Things continued, of
course, to develop on all fronts. Casualties Union's own

competitions had become so popular that at the beginning of 1950 it was announced that there was no reason to bar either doctors or nurses from teams competing in the Buxton Trophy Competition.

We were greatly encouraged by an announcement that the War Office had issued a general instruction that Territorial R.A.M.C. training was in future to be on Casualties Union lines.

16

More Changes at the Top

In late 1947, Brigadier W. Rowley Bristow completed his term of office as president and handed over to a colleague, with whom he had been associated in neighbouring theatres of war, Brigadier St John D. Buxton, M.B., B.S., F.R.C.S. Mr St John Buxton became a very great friend and benefactor to Casualties Union and opened his presidency with a message to all our members.

'Members of Casualties Union deserve great appreciation for their work in developing a method of teaching and practising first-aid. There is enormous scope, not only for the spectacle of a serious train or 'bus accident, but also for the injury or sudden physical catastrophe in the factory or home. The necessity for training in first-aid should be realized by everyone who reads the newspapers, in which are recorded road accidents and air and train catastrophes. No one knows where such may occur, so the societies responsible for the training in first-aid aim at having instruction centres all over the country. Hence it is imperative to spread the influence of the union.

'Recruits are required from all over this country and many more centres will enable the work of Casualties Union to go hand in hand with the instruction of first-aid. The high standard of the instructors has made a great impression on me and they realize that many others of equal ability and originality must be trained to provide the ideal service in Great Britain.

'In sending this message — one of congratulations and encouragement — I cannot close without reference to the death of your last president, Mr W. Rowley Bristow. He was a brilliant surgeon, excellent organizer in peace and war and his spoken word always gave confidence to those working in any organization with which he was associated. Good luck; work hard; keep the standard up; spread news of Casualties Union's work.'

Over the next few years, as the open competitions in first-aid and diagnosis became increasingly popular, our president gave us three trophies for annual competition. Firstly the Buxton Trophy which is held for one year by the team in the open competition gaining the highest aggregate marks in first-aid and diagnosis. As the interest grew enough for teams from other countries to compete in our competitions, an international contest was developed in which all the casualties spoke a language unintelligible to any of the teams. It was a language devised by a lady from Australia, who belonged to our Reading branch. There was also a great interest shown by juniors and to include them in the programme a junior competition was created. Mr Buxton generously presented trophies for each of these, known as the International Buxton Trophy and the Junior Buxton Trophy respectively.

In 1952, Brigadier Buxton was succeeded by Major-General Philip H. Mitchener, C.B., C.B.E., T.D., Army Medical Service; Vice-President, Royal College of Surgeons; a man of great distinction. I had been privileged to meet Philip Mitchiner, while both of us were serving in the senior O.T.C. I was a sergeant in the sappers and he was then Colonel commanding the Medical Wing. We came into contact when I was on duty as Brigade Orderly Sergeant and some of the medicos were in difficulties over tents and marquees that would not stay up in a violent storm with heavy rain and winds. I remember his delight as I recalled the event to him when I called upon him to invite him to accept nomination as our president. When in due course he took office, he sent the following message to the members.

'I feel that in assuming the responsibilities of president of Casualties Union, which I do with a mixture of pleasure and trepidation, I am likely to prove but an unworthy successor to that very good friend whom I have known since our service together in the First World War in Salonica, Brigadier Buxton. Buxton is a man whose charm of personality, whose knowledge of surgery and orthopaedics, and whose sympathetic consideration of the problems of all with whom he comes in contact, make it exceedingly difficult to succeed in an appointment which he valued greatly and in which we have to thank him for his unstinted service during his period in office.

'I look forward during my presidency to meeting the members of Casualties Union, with the value of whose work I am already acquainted through having attended both Combatent Service, Red Cross and St John Ambulance Brigade competitions. I have long realized that the services of Casualties Union in providing realism have been of inestimable value in stimulating the interest and sense of reality on all these occasions. It is a very different thing to be faced by a skilled 'made-up' casualty to having to try to imagine that an obviously normal individual represents a blood-stained mess, and I am well aware how adequately the trained members of Casualties Union can realistically imitate, all apart from their make-up, the condition of a casualty in any condition.

'I am looking forward at the first week-end of October to meeting a large number of members from all over the country, though I fear that it is unlikely that our Johannesburg branch will be able to be represented. What a pity we have not

73

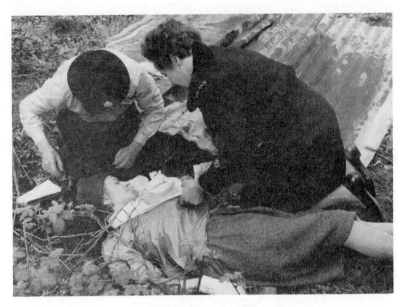

Civil Defence training

branches in other Dominions and Colonies.'
PHILIP H. MITCHENER

At this time in my capacity as the chairman of the council, I enunciated for the first time the target for which the union was striving:

> 'It is the aim of Casualties Union that ultimately there shall be trained 'casualties' to assist wherever first aid is taught.'

The union insists upon its members being TRAINED to act as casualties so that their behaviour may be medically accurate and consistent throughout (with due allowance for the effects of handling, treatment and changing circumstances). First aiders handling such 'patients' can gain experience which is seriously misleading. (I mention this to draw attention to the dangers of using make-up, however well done, upon untrained patients.) They will fail to emphasize the care that is required in the handling of injured persons, because they will not show appropriate pain, distress, and deterioration of condition when wrongly handled or treated, nor the appropriate degreee of improvement under correct treatment. It will also be appreciated that in some circumstances it will be totally impossible to avoid hurting a patient and it is imperative that the 'patient' should be able to express pain and the general effect that it produces on his condition.

It was a stupendous task. Hence my inclusion of the word Ultimately.

We were very conscious of the debt we owed to the members of the medical profession who supervised the training locally and advised us on technical matters. It was, and of course still is, absolutely essential that the appearance, behaviour and situation of every 'casualty' should be medically consistent, and we relied upon our friends in the medical profession to keep us right.

It followed that there could never be ready-made situations in which stereotyped casualties behave in a stereotyped manner. There is no substitute for the training laid down by the union which gathers together the fund of major and minor experience which every human being has behind him, adds to it the experience of others, the advice, criticism of the doctor, nurses and fellow 'casualties' and serves it up with the experience of being 'injured', 'trapped' and 'rescued'. A 'casualty' so trained is able to respond to the ever-changing situation that develops during the handling of a first aid incident.

About this time too we appeared in a supporting role to the British Red Cross Society on B.B.C. television in Women's Hour. The producer of the programme, For Women, approached the B.R.C.S. to give a fortnightly series of talks and demonstrations on simple first aid in the home. One of the society's medical advisers was to give the talks and a woman member of the organization to demonstrate the practical treatment. Casualties Union was asked to provide the patients. The audience would be composed of all types of women, possibly alone in a house or maybe watching with small children (under school age). It was important that the B.B.C.s responsibility should be properly appreciated — the talks were not intended for first aiders.

The subjects chosen were those that the average person, ignorant of medical knowledge, should be able to deal with if confronted with them when no immediate help was available. They included shock, sprains and strains, cuts and grazes, burns and scalds, foreign bodies in eye, nose and ear and electric shock and asphyxia.

The B.B.C. were insistent that the presentation must be toned down sufficiently to be helpful and not to frighten the possibly nervous adult or child. It was therefore somewhat gratifying when in the third talk on cuts and grazes quite a lot of 'blood' was allowed to be shown.

Everything was rehearsed — not once only but several times! There was an initial reading through of scripts with assistant producers, doctor and member of B.R.C.S. at the doctor's surgery, where any complications were ironed out and corrections made where necessary, usually followed by a second run through after correction.

The doctor, presenter, first aider and patient then had a few days in which to become thoroughly acquainted with their respective parts, and finally came a dress rehearsal on the morning of the 'show'. A ten to fifteen minute item entailed several hours work at least. On the day itself it meant arriving at the studio at 10 am and not leaving before 4.30 pm.

The importance of 'timing' was a headache peculiar to television, as cameras had to pick up alternately the doctor, presenter, who were speaking, and the patient and the first aider who were acting. All this had to be perfected through considerable rehearsal, and meticulous care over the slightest detail. It was in fact a splendid exposition of the principle of Casualties Union that only the very best is good enough — we are concerned with saving other peoples' lives.

17

Tenth Anniversary

As we approached our tenth anniversary our president used his influence to gain us an invitation to hold a celebration dinner at the Royal College of Surgeons. We made our plans and as the time drew near our president himself died. It was unthinkable that we should rejoice under such circumstances, so we asked if we might postpone the occasion to a later date. Our friend and former President St J.D. Buxton returned briefly into office until we could appoint a successor. He kindly wrote the following obituary:

P.H. MITCHINER, C.B., C.B.E., T.D.
Vice-President, Royal College of Surgeons;
Major-General, A.M.S.; Professor of Surgery;
President of Casualties Union.

Members of Casualties Union have had little opportunity of knowing Major-General Mitchiner, as it was only a short time ago that he was appointed President. Although he has had impaired health recently, the news of his death was as unexpected as it was distressing — in fact, he was due to give an important lecture a few days later.

By profession he was a surgeon, and like others of this age he had given many years to affairs of the Army Medical Services. He studied at St

Thomas' Hospital and acquired the highest degrees in medicine and surgery awarded by the University of London, as well as the Fellowship of the Royal College of Surgeons. Appointed to the surgical staff of his hospital, it soon became apparent that he was a brilliant and amusing teacher and an indefatigable surgeon. All his life he talked and taught common sense based on his own academic and practical experience. He was not interested in rules and regulations, particularly if they gave prominence to authority not fully conversant with local conditions.

His ability and professional success were recognized by his fellows, so that he was on the council of the Royal College of Surgeons and held high office in the University.

I think our first meeting was in an O.T.C. camp before the first war. His peacetime and wartime services were extensive and brought him many friends as well as high honours. After our first meeting on Salisbury Plain we never served in the same unit, but met in several countries where he was serving as consultant, surgical adviser or administrator. He knew the Balkans and the Middle East, but possibly enjoyed his service in England equally well. It would be out of place here to go in detail into his work in each sphere. The qualities of Philip Mitchiner were not primarily connected with his work, but were human ones. His cheerful greeting, the healthy encouragement and possibly kindly reproof — so typical of the man — were good for all of us and I think he knew we loved him for each one of them. The twinkle of youth in his eye, which he never lost, was familiar to his friends.

Casualties Union has lost a man who would have endeared himself to every member, and I know was anxious to be a useful officer of committee and President of the Union.

St J.D.B.

78

In the circumstances it was decided to defer our celebrations until we had appointed a new president and the Royal College of Surgeons kindly agreed to a postponement rather than a cancellation. In the meantime many messages of congratulation and best wishes reached the union from many quarters.

On the tenth anniversay of Casualties Union I send you greetings and encouragement for your future activities.

St J.D. BUXTON
Past President and Acting President of the Union

I can remember, a long time ago as it seems now, when I first came across the magnificent work being evolved at Leatherhead and how impressed I was with its great value to Civil Defence training. I have watched the developments all the way through with the greatest interest, and it has been particularly pleasing to see how the work of Casualties Union has spread, not only over Britain but outside this country as well. I was especially interested to see a demonstration in Canada last time I was over there in July.

I am quite certain that the techniques developed are of the utmost importance and I can only hope that the splendid work, which has of course the greatest value for peace as well as for war, will go on from strength to strength.

SIR JOHN HODSOLL
Home Office (Civil Defence Department)

Some four years ago the British Red Cross Society and Casualties Union began to collaborate closely to their mutual benefit.

The value of their efforts was well illustrated by the remark made by a young member who helped to render First Aid to the victims of the recent accident at the Farnborough Air Display, and who said: 'If I had not been trained on casualties provided by our Casualties Union Study Circle I could not possibly have coped with the injuries I met.'

THE BRITISH RED CROSS SOCIETY

Sitting on the harbour wall at Padstow trying to remember the signs and symptoms of the various conditions of unconsiousness for a first aid examination, I felt greatly the need for visual demonstration.

Then I saw a Diagnosis Test staged by Casualties Union, in which twelve patients, each illustrating a condition of unconsciousness, were acting the symptoms and showing the signs.

I realized immediately that here was the answer for which I had been looking.

I am satisfied that first aid, which must in the nature of things be given unexpectedly, can be effective only if the first aiders have rehearsed the treatment under realistic conditions in which the patients are made up for the part and acting it.

In this the tenth year of your existence I am satisfied that Casualties Union has a great and useful part to play in helping the voluntary societies to teach First Aid.

MAJOR-GENERAL L.A. HAWES
British Red Cross Society

The first ten years of a new movement are always full of interest, especially when it is as revolutionary as Casualties Union. How many lives have been lost because of the lack of realistic instructions in first-aid and rescue work! Having broken, at various times, samples of most of my bones, it has often given me cold shudders to see what happens at first-aid demonstrations; in fact, I always advise Scouts that before they start operations they should make sure that the victim is disarmed! Casualties Union, born in the days of the war to meet this need, has revolutionized the whole of first-aid training. The tremendous enthusiasm, imagination and skill of the pioneers has overcome

Scouts to the rescue

Photo by courtesy of Isle of Thanet Gazette

all obstacles. Their devotion to the task has led to branches being formed, not only all over the United Kingdom, but in several of the overseas Dominions and Colonies. The need for such a movement is not confined to war. In the disasters and hazards of peace-time, in factory, mine, flood and tempest, the work that they have done and are doing will continue to earn the gratitude of the victims. We, in Scouting, are proud to think that it was an Old Scout who first had the idea, and that many members of our Movement are to be found in your ranks. May the next ninety be as fruitful as the first ten!

ROWALLEN
Chief Scout

Here are good and sincere wishes from Canada for the continued success of Casualties Union, on the occasion of their Tenth Birthday. Such devoted work, as 'something extra' in the field of First Aid training, cannot fail to be honoured and valued wherever it becomes known. Best of luck go with you all!

MAJOR RICHARD BINGHAM
Director, Civil Service Civil Defence, Ottawa

I hope you will accept our best wishes for the future, and our congratulations for the work you have done in the past ten years, not only in England, but also in Holland. Please interpret these wishes to the whole Council and to all mambers of the Union.

B.D.C. van MANNEN
Eindhoven, Holland

Rangering does not specialize in First Aid, but aims at giving the girls elementary knowledge of how to cope with an emergency until trained help arrives. Where a girl shows interest in First Aid and Nursing she is encouraged to attend either British Red Cross or St John Ambulance Brigade lectures. The Company whose Captain is a member, or who has friends who are members, of a Casualties Union Study Circle, gain valuable assistance and confidence in dealing with an emergency, if they have had the co-operation with a trained 'acting casualty'. No book knowledge or 'labelled' patient will teach a girl how to handle injured people. We thank Casualties Union for their tremendous help, and hope for even greater co-operation in the coming years.

MISS V.A. LAWRENCE
Ranger Branch, Girl Guide Association

At the tenth annual reunion of Casualties Union, Mr Paterson (the guest of honour) remarked that what had impressed him most at the demonstration was the spirit of confidence that pervaded it.

To my mind, he could not have chosen a happier or more apt word than 'confidence' as this exemplifies the whole organization and activities of Casualties Union. It was confidence in himself and his ideal which inspired Mr E.C. Claxton, as Commandant of the Rescue Training School at Leatherhead in 1942, to realize that an organization such as Casualties Union was badly needed as an adjunct to the training in First Aid. It was the supreme confidence in him and this ideal of a devoted band of helpers at the school which enabled him to formulate the system of training by the 'faking' of injuries upon live 'casualties', and teaching them to act the parts they were supposed to play as such.

Up to that time methods of teaching First Aid had been dull and unrealistic, but Mr Claxton and Casualties Union revolutionized all that and laid the foundation of an organization which has gone from strength to strength to reach the high standard of excellence to which it has attained today. I have no hesitation in saying that it has proved and is proving, of inestimable value in connection with the teaching of First Aid, and further, has become a benefit to humanity in general.

I had the pleasure and privilege of first coming into contact with Casualties Union in 1943 when as a member of the headquarters Staff for Casualty Services at the Ministry of Health and Home Office, I was invited to visit the Rescue Training School at Leatherhead. Since that time I have been fortunate in being able to maintain close contact with the Union and its activities, and am proud and grateful to have been made one of its Honorary Members.

It has been a great pleasure to me to be able to attend the annual reunions and meet old friends, amongst whom are some of the founders of the organization. I wish the Union all the success which it so richly deserves.

(Dr) E.S. GOSS

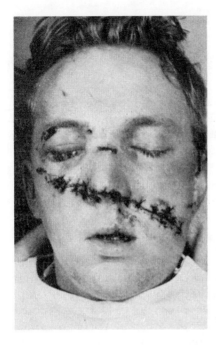

How realistic
can you get?

On this, the tenth anniversary of Casualties Union, may I, as one who has unfortunately retired from active membership, send you all my heart-felt greetings and congratualtions on the attainment of your tenth birthday? For many of you, it has been ten very active years of blood, sweat and not a few tears, enjoyed in the spirit of self-sacrifice perhaps unparalelled in the history of voluntary service. Fortified with the knowledge that your skill and ever-increasing ability is making a major contribution to the alleviation of human suffering, you must, and will, press on with even greater determination in the years to come.

F.H. LOWE

The last ten years have proved for all who care to take notice that the work of Casualties Union, with its sound principles, ingenious technique and enthusiastic application by its members, represents the most important contribution to first-aid training of its time. It will attract and instruct the beginner, serve as a reliable basis for tests of competence, and provide the qualified with a stimulus to further study.

Born in the years of the war, Casualties Union has daily chances of proving its worth for the immediate treatment of the still growing numbers of traffic, industrial and home accidents. Its work deserves the permanent support of the authorities and organizations concerned with the prevention of avoidable mistakes in First Aid. Members are earning the gratitude of all who through their efforts are spared unnecessary complications in the treatment of their injuries, not least of all the doctors, whose task is rendered easier by their skill.

(Dr) L.S. MICHAELIS

I would like you to accept, on behalf of our Circle, our congratulations on your tenth Birthday. You should know how proud we feel to be associated with you, and we send our very best wishes for the future.

MRS McLINTOCK
Study Circle S.A.7, Johannesburg

Casualties Union completes ten years of existence and seven of peacetime activities. I hope that every member is proud of the position and standing of the Union today, and proud of what has been accomplished in the past ten years and of the ever-widening area of its activities.

From the bewildered uncertainty of the immediate post-war conditions has been built up a solid foundation of enterprise, initiative and achievement. The principles for which the Union stands are now generally accepted: it provides casualties for practically all the important first-aid competitions in the country, and is being used for training in an ever widening field, in civilian life, in the Services, and even in the nursing profession.

Continuing effort and experiment is necessary to keep ahead of all followers and to fulfil what is probably the real function of Casualties Union: that it shall be the fountain-head of knowledge and instruction in the art of casualty interpretation.

Satisfaction without complacency must be our watchword. The real importance of our work is only just beginning to be realized. The scope is ever widening.

One thing above all gives cause for satisfaction: the old wonderful spirit of cameraderie, of endeavour and of adventure continues undimmed. May it always do so. It must carry Casualties Union from strength to strength, overcoming all difficulties.

(Dr) J.E. HAINE

18

Conference 1952

In this tenth year we staged the first Casualties Union Conference on Saturday, 4 October, 1952, at Holme House, Bedford College, Regents Park, London, with some sixty members present. The chair was taken by Mr Harry Davies, chairman of the general committee, who welcomed the members and then introduced me. I explained the tremendous change that had been brought about since the end of the war. I said that in the wartime days my leadership was, of necessity, a dictatorship. After the war ended the union became a democratic organization with its council and committee, and has continued along those lines. It was the desire of the committee that the conference should record its observations and make suggestions for future development.

The first speaker was Mrs Helen Nicholson on the subject of 'holding of preliminary regional rounds for the annual competition and regional competitions'. Our speaker outlined the feeling which, she said, for some time had been exercising the minds of many, that some of the burden of organization of the competition should be carried by others — or, as she aptly put it, 'headquarters must be able to pass on the baton in the relay race'. One of the greatest inducements to teams entering Casualties Union competitions was that of entering a new field of conquest outside their own orbit and on neutral ground.

In their own regions the teams became familiar with each other and with the judges and the problems that they offered. In other words a regional competition must be run on the same lines as the finals in London.

Mr Percy Sargeant spoke on the subject of 'widening the membership' and suggested that the time had come when some other form of membership was desirable and, indeed, necessary. More people than ever before were now training in casualty representation either within the union or in the first aid organizations themselves. All those who trained with Study Circle methods did not join the union as members. Were those people to be allowed to lose touch with us? What of those who trained in their own societies? might not they be allowed to participate in some form of membership? Mr Sargeant thought that the Union was fast becoming an institution in the art of realistic portrayal, and it should be deemed a qualification and privilege to obtain a certificate under our auspices. Could the union offer degrees of fellowship, so that those who take their training under other organizations attain a licentiate qualification?

Mr Sargeant concluded with the comment that there was much to be thought over and discussed along these lines and he hoped that branches and study circles would give them much consideration.

Mrs E.L. (Steve) Eaton, who as secretary of the conference sub-committee, had made a great contribution towards the mounting of this first conference, was our next speaker. Steve addressed the meeting on the difficult subject of training the isolated recruit which she said should be linked with the contact so essential for the isolated member. She contended that the difficulties of training alone on the Study Circle lines were almost insuperable and emphasised that whilst it was difficult enough to practise make-up and faking alone or with an untrained relative, it was impossible to act and react alone. One had no criticism and so no standard could be achieved. Steve queried whether it might be possible to have some simplified form of training with a different examination and certificates in such cases, possibly an associate's certificate? Could a much reduced capitation fee be introduced for isolated cases or for small groups up to three? Concerning isolated members (of whom roughly forty already existed on the register) Steve suggested refresher courses at regional, not branch, level, and

Mrs E.L. (Steve) Eaton

particularly one annually in the London area, possibly in conjunction with the annual competition, to make it worth taking a journey for a weekend for those who lived some little distance away. She was aware that this idea would be unpopular with headquarters because of the extra work entailed at the same time as the competition, but thought that could be overcome by making the refresher course the sole responsibility of instructors and members, not senior instructors, thereby, at the same time, finding a possible pool for potential senior instructors. Bravo Steve!

From the floor, Dr MacFadyen, of Stirling Study Circle, suggested that in the case of the isolated recruit the First Aid Society organizing the local first aid course should be approached to start a Study Circle. Mrs Anderson suggested that centres be allotted for refresher courses.

The chairman closed that part of the proceedings, apologizing for being behind time and announced that a demonstration of practical work would start immediately, to be followed at 12.30 pm by the presentation of a film strip on war injuries, to be presented by Lieutenant-Colonel E.S.

Goss, M.C., M.R.C.S.

The demonstrations included the 'new bread' technique for major swelling as in a sprained ankle by Miss Nancy Budgett. Mr Connolly, also of Cranleigh, showed how he faked a closed fracture of the lower leg so that when roughly handled the bone broke through the skin, creating an open fracture. Members of Warrington Study Circle showed the cleansing of a dirty wound. Misses Philbrick and Bowring from Cornwall specialized in creating false tissues, while Mr P. Ask of Berkshire built up a stitchable 'wound' and one of the doctors obliged by suturing it then and there. This latter caused a lot of interest. As earlier other demonstrations were crowded out by lack of time, so we had to go without Mr Cyril Wallis's 'bloods' and Mrs Brenda Whiteley's faces until later.

The evening session was chaired by Major-General L.A. Hawes, O.B.E., D.S.O, M.C., vice-president of the union, who opened the proceedings by the showing of a film made during the year and now shown for the first time. It was unedited and clearly needed much cutting but showed some splendid work in staging both simple and complex situations. Mrs Nicholson who presented the film was warmly congratulated on the initiative which had created this opportunity.

The chairman then introduced Miss Ina Robb, of Glasgow Study Circle 94; her subject 'Additional facilities required for the Study Circle Scheme'. Outlining the advantages already in operation she praised in particular the work of Mrs Nicholson, assistant Study Circle secretary, who was unstinting in her efforts, and she always answered a letter by return. Passing on suggestions, she said she thought a little less spoon-feeding might do good. She also felt that a common pool was needed to which circles and branches could send ideas for the use of others. Finally, she thought a field day once a year was the greatest possible help. All Study Circles and branches in the area could meet at this and if possible a member from headquarters should be present so that new ideas could be presented.

The delegate from Rotherham Study Circle, Mr E. Hedge, then presented his ideas on the same subject, by asking why we had to commence a conference in the morning and show the practical demonstrations before lunch (for which he could not arrive in time) then leave the afternoon vacant. He followed this complaint by stating that he would like to see more practical work done by the senior instructors — more demonstrations by them. He would like closer co-operation between Study Circles, and regional grouping should be encouraged. Another idea of his concerned the wonderful record headquarters must possess of knowledge and experience — a pool of information would be invaluable. Could not extracts from the record of activities sheets be put at the disposal of such a pool? The marking sheets for examination of candidates could be useful in showing up weaknesses and enable the circle to concentrate on improvement where it was needed. Such marking sheets should be explicit in their criticisms and be available to the Study Circle afterwards. Rotherham would keep a book for doctors and senior instructors to write comments on work done.

The chairman thanked both speakers for their helpful talks and emphasised the salient points for discussion. There were a number of comments from the floor. One Circle was using the record of activity forms for criticisms from doctors — they asked the doctor to write his opinion on the back of the form.

Requests were made for a senior instructor to be present at examinations as well as doctors. Several members felt that doctors were often too easily impressed by the technique and were not always critical enough.

Some already kept books of cuttings from newspapers, etc., re accidents, and Mr Claxton drew attention to a publication by the Home Office Inspector of Factories on 'How Accidents Happen'. This was available from Casualties Union library.

Mr Roy Stokes reminded members that ideas for publication in the journal were needed and if they were not fully written up it did not matter — the editor promised to 'knock them into shape'.

Mr Claxton spoke on the problems of branch and regional development. Firstly, he warned members not to appear to do things outside the union's province — differences between Casualties Union and other organizations could so much more easily be ironed out at an early stage if we had strong organized groups in each area. He emphasised the need for the union to maintain its status as a separate and independent organization to which all first aid bodies could turn for help, and hoped to see the development of more branches to this end.

These could eventually coalesce into regions so that the various branches could assist each other by providing instructors for examinations in the other branches. Much as senior instructors would like to travel and help, the expense factor must be borne in mind. He referred to the question of members leaving their First Aid Society after joining Casualties Union. This was often wrongly attributed to Casualties Union. He was pleased that the Study Circles asked for more criticism — only by improving standards, rather than trying to maintain them, would we progress. Headquarters had some fourteen senior instructors, who had also to be office workers. More senior instructors were needed. The greatest difficulty from the headquarters aspect was expense.

Comments from the floor underlined that regional organization would need money for postage, travel, etc., although the maximum value of training for money expended would be by regional organization.

And so to the open forum. A member criticised the acting in the film shown earlier and a doctor suggested the use of a professional or even good amateur producer or actor to help on this side of the work. Mrs Whiteley replied by saying that experience had shown this to be of very little use. Another member reinforced her remarks by saying that they had started training under an amateur producer for a time, and only when they had 'got rid of her' had they managed to produce results. Mr Harry Davies and Mrs Nicholson both emphasised the need for the actor to 'live the part'.

A meeting of Study Circle leaders and secretaries would be a helpful idea. In answer to questions about the admissibility and advisability of using juniors in demonstrations and of providing incidents for juniors, Mr Claxton warned members that parents' permission should always be obtained before juniors were used. Discretion was needed in the case of demonstrating technique to youngsters — it should be kept simple and not frighten or distress in any way.

The chairman, Major-General Hawes, then brought the proceedings to an end by illustrating from personal experience at Barnett Hill how Casualties Union could bring the First Aid Book to life, and how much the 'blooding' of members of first aid organizations by realistic portrayal could help the first aider for the sights seen and the nervous strain felt when first meeting with a bad accident. In particular he quoted the calm and control shown by Red Cross workers in the Farnborough disaster. He was convinced that Casualties Union must go on as an independent body and was inclined to see the future of the union as the teaching body for casualty acting and make-up. With regard to any difficulties which might occur when a Casualties Union circle, which had grown from a division or detachment in a First Aid Society, wished to work with another organization — he was sure that no trouble would arise if the Study Circle leader would inform his or her county headquarters of what was wished. He concluded by thanking, on behalf of the audience and himself, the organizers of the conference. Whereupon Mr Claxton rose to express the thanks of all to General Hawes for his able chairmanship and his helpful remarks.

19

Eric Claxton Visits the North-East Region in 1952

I was delighted when I managed to arrange to take a week of my summer leave visiting some of the branches in Yorkshire, Durham and Northumberland. It was difficult to fix a week which suited all the groups I wanted to visit but somehow they all contrived to arrange their plans so that I could meet as many of the members as possible. It was my first tour of the kind, and one that I shall long remember. I had been impressed by their goodwill in trying to fit into the pattern to make a convenient itinerary for me. I was even more impressed by the warmth of the welcome which awaited me and by the initiative, enthusiasm and skill displayed by every group.

In Hull, the Kingston branch had staged a series of incidents in the docks. Two 'casualties' had been injured during the shunting of railway waggons and another had fallen into the hold of a lighter. Such incidents as these provide excellent training and the City Ambulance Service collaborated with the assistance of wireless-controlled ambulances. Police teams dealt with the situations. Mr. Bromfield and his Branch were doing valuable work.

The Cottingham branch staged a contrasting demonstration at the St. John Headquarters, where another police team cleared up another situation which had happened in a garden. The careful and patient attention to detail made it hard to believe that the garden had been created upon the stage of a hall. Grass, crazy paving, borders of flowers,

94

cloches, tea in the garden and all the garden furniture and garden implements were there, complete. After this situation had been dealt with, there was a valuable diagnosis exercise to complete the show. One was impressed by the support of the Red Cross, St. John, City Ambulance, Police and Youth Services and I would like to pay tribute to Miss E.H. Browne, who was leader of the first Study Circle ever formed and who achieved such a high standard and gained such prestige in the area.

On to Darlington and to a first class display by the branch who were helping to 'decorate' the new St. John Headquarters. They had contrived a series of accidents in the process, all of which could have happened, and I felt a genuine distress for some of the victims who suffered most realistically. Since this was the passing-out test for a number of probationers, the high standard was particularly gratifying. This feeling was obviously shared by the two doctors who observed their performance with me. Some of these members had only a few days before provided the casualties for the final stage of the National Coal Board Competition. They are a grand team under the leadership of Mr. H. Carr.

And so to Newcastle for the weekend course for instructors. This was mainly in the capable hands of Mrs. H. M. Nicholson, but there was no doubt that the branch committee had put an enormous amount of preparatory work into the excellent arrangements. The way that the City Corporation and lay public responded to their requests showed in what esteem the branch was held locally.

Miss N. M. Budgett and Mr. A. C. Wallis, of headquarters had travelled to Newcastle to assist on this course, and guests from other branches had come from Glasgow, Warrington, Hull, Rotherham and Rowlands Gill. A number of instructor candidates successfully passed their practical tests, and afterwards the shooting of a very ambitious film was undertaken. I must confess that I had many doubts whether the project was too ambitious, but the way the members of the course rallied to the exacting demands of the moving camera dispelled my doubts as soon as the operation started. The work of shooting was undertaken by a member of the Newcastle Amateur

'There's a man alive under here!'

Cinematograph Society with a magnificent camera. I hoped the final results would fully justify the effort made by the branch and their friends.

While I was in Newcastle I was invited to meet the Whitley Bay St. John Faking Group. This group had its beginning in Study Circles 105 and 106, and it was a great pleasure to meet them and to see the work they are doing under the leadership of one of our instructors, Miss Joyce Fearnside. I hoped they would keep in touch with the union, because we all had so much to learn from each other's experiences.

On my return journey I visited the Study Circle at Easingwold, which was doing such useful work at the Home Office Civil Defence School. Commander Austin, the director of the school, paid high tribute to their work and said he considered that rescue training needed first-class trained 'casualties'.

The circle staged a series of accidents in the house,

garden, orchard and coachyard of the home of Mrs. Scott. This group was indeed fortunate to have such a leader, for she has tremendous energy and initiative. Although many of the 'casualties' were only probationers they put on a remarkable demonstration. There was much valuable material there and I formed the impression that the circle had a great future. They had courage, initiative, enthusiasm and a lot of talent.

And so with a glad heart I returned to London, happy to know that the spirit that created Casualties Union had been conveyed by the Study Circle Scheme to all these groups so far away. They were selfless in their service and anxious only to do as well as possible. Everywhere I was asked for my criticisms; I was frankly torn between giving none and so encouraging weaknesses, and drawing attention to faults and so leaving the impression behind me that the members were less good than they really were. I chose the latter course in an endeavour to give constructive criticism and I may have been unduly tough.

20

Road Safety Week in Farnham, Surrey

(As reported in the *Farnham Herald* — 8th August, 1952)

Three accidents in one morning and within the space of one and a half hours! Luckily they were all 'staged', and though they looked most realistic they were acted merely to bring home to the public the necessity for care, and to show how easy it is for them to happen. They were part of Farnham's Road Safety Week programme.

First, a woman driver in Castle Street suddenly opened the door of her car without looking to see if anything was coming. In doing so she knocked a cyclist off his machine, causing him head injuries and a laceration to the arm. She herself had her leg crushed in the door of her car and suffered from shock, while a woman passer-by fainted. Three casualties through one act of thoughtlessness.

The second 'accident' happened in West Street opposite the post office. Here a woman tried to pass in front of a car and was knocked down by another. Result (according to schedule) fracture of clavicle and head injuries.

The third was staged in South Street opposite to the cattle market, where a boy cyclist riding carelessly came into collision with another boy

98

walking aimlessly. The scheduled injuries due to this accident were 'compound fracture of tibia and fibula and a Collis fracture and serious abrasions'.

Figuring in these three 'accidents' were members of Casualties Union, a voluntary organization set up some ten years ago by Mr. E. C. Claxton, who was then in charge of the Surrey County Civil Defence Rescue School at Leatherhead. The accidents are 'staged' very cleverly, and those taking part are extremely true to life, whether as casualties or accident-causers.

Just how realistic has been the acting can be judged from the fact that a gentleman approached the car under which the woman was lying in the second 'accident' and offered to help lift the car and started to do so. It took quite a lot of explanation on the part of Inspector Loveridge to convince him it was just 'acting'.

21

Official Opening of Hampshire County C.D. Training School and Ground

To coincide with the granting of branch status, Southampton engaged in their most interesting and largest operation, which happened incidentally to involve the type of work for which Casualties Union was originally formed. The occasion was the official opening of Hampshire's Civil Defence Training School and Ground.

After the opening ceremony, demonstrations were staged; firstly the combined fire-gas chamber and then the gas compound for the detection of liquid mustard gas and the secret nerve gas found in Germany after the war.

Finally an incident on the 'training set' — a pair of specially constructed semi-detached houses suitably demolished to represent bomb damage. This was our job in conjunction with twenty wardens, rescue party, W.V.S., police and Ambulance Service.

Bombs had fallen and these occupied houses had been hit; the wardens arrived and (to quote a report):

'A man and a woman, their eyes staring vacantly, their faces covered with blood, staggered from the rubble of the bombed building. Air raid wardens ran to their assistance. Then all lay flat as a series of deafening explosions caused more damage and started a fire in the building. Another man came into view from the devastated area, covered with dust. He fell forward, clutching his chest, coughing and spitting blood.

'At the same time wardens were in the buildings, where they had located further casualties, and incidentally two casualties occurred amongst the wardens as a result of the second stick of bombs.

'In one house, occupied by a man with his wife and child, the wife in the front room downstairs was trapped by the leg under a door and other debris (severe crush injury to leg and shock), the child near her was suffering from shock but was not trapped. A warden had just located them when further bombs were dropped (lacerated forehead). The husband was in the upstairs back room, the only part of the upper floor left in either house (severe facial cuts and abrasions, severely lacerated arm, minor cuts and abrasions to legs and body, and shock).

'Buried casualties were thought to be in the next house, so the rescue party had been sent for and in the meantime surface casualties in the first house were dealt with and removed. In the other house, a mother and son were completely buried in the downstair front room, while her sister was covered with debris in the back room; a warden had a fractured clavicle, caused by a falling beam in the second bomb attack; and in this house a fire occurred which had to be dealt with before the casualties could be located.

'The mother and son were buried together under the complete top floor debris and when found and rescued the following injuries were revealed. Mother, compound fracture tibia and severely lacerated leg with arterial haemmorhage, which did not commence to bleed freely until casualty was located and compression on leg removed. The son, crushed hand and fractured radius and ulna. Sister, severely crushed foot.'

This was a very interesting and instructive job which we all thoroughly enjoyed even if there were discomforts, for some of the casualties were 'under ground' for about forty-five minutes. We were certainly grateful to the W.V.S., for it really was hot and sweet tea the patients received for their shock treatment.

22

*Eric Claxton is Casualty in Exercise
in the City of Westminster*

I was briefed to play the unspectacular part of a dead body
at a rehearsal for a combined Civil Defence Services
demonstration and took up my position amongst the muck
and debris of a particularly shattered building in a road
that had been damaged by enemy action and now, in
peace-time, served as a training ground for the new Civil
Defence Corps.

The rescuers knew that they had a dead body to recover
from within and I waited as the darkness grew, getting
colder and at the same time trying to settle into a
convincing position which I could maintain without
difficulty after I had grown more numbed. I could hear
outside the scuffle of feet and the sound of vehicles and
above the clang of fire engines ringing their bells I heard
the commentator instructing the spectators about the
situation.

Gradually an acrid smell of smoke reached my nostrils
and I tried to discipline my breathing so that there should
be no tell-tale heaving of my chest. It was quite dark now
and my limbs were growing cold and numb. Suddenly there
was a rush of heavy boots as the door was bashed in and I
guessed by the orders given that the fire service had come to
extinguish the fire four floors up. As the men leapt up the
stairs with lines of hose and, worse still, as they leapt down
again, the dust added to the fumes of the fire, demanding

all my self-control to control my breathing. I wanted deep breaths and I wanted to cough.

Then a senior man came in and asked: 'What's that there?' and someone replied: 'Don't mind that, it's a corpse.' 'Well, go steady! There are no dummies this time — they are all real,' and so saying he shone the powerful beam of his torch straight onto my face. I was holding my eyes closed but even so it was most uncomfortable and I had to steel myself once more to avoid flinching. They were stamping around me causing the planks to vibrate unpleasantly and drive the grit into my inert face lying on the boards. I was very grateful to someone who said: 'Mind you don't tread on his fingers.' Such kindness was a help, though I was not comforted when someone else remarked: 'Well, he's dead anyway, he can wait.'

A spray of water from one of the hoses — I learnt afterwards that there were four of them up the stairs near my head — spattered over my head and I was again hard put to it to remain inert, but it was a comfort because it laid the dust and made the prolonged wait less unpleasant.

At last there was a fresh group of feet coming in my direction — the rescue men had come to collect me. They, too, knew that I was dead, though they pulled me about to find where I'd been hurt and then pronounced that I was dead. To my surprise when a stretcher was brought I was invited to 'be a sport and get onto the stretcher for us,' but I lay quite still and was very careful not to breathe. They picked me up with kindly hands and rolled me onto a stretcher in a blanket. This gave me a chance to take two good breaths without being seen, which helped a lot. 'Better cover his face up with the blanket since we haven't a shroud,' said someone; and again I was grateful, for it helped to warm me and also keep the lights and grit out of my eyes.

As we came out into the night air, stumbling across the debris, the commentator was still instructing the audience. He said that the dead would eventually be removed in a mortuary van but were being placed temporarily out of sight to prevent lowering morale. On arrival at the temporary halt there was a checking between warden and rescue as to where I'd been found and who I was. To my fresh surprise I was taken by the shoulders and propped up in a sitting position. 'Come on! I've checked you off, you can go home now,' was his comment, but I had to wait for the mortuary van, so still inert I flopped back onto the stretcher. It was a draughty passage and the warden was eager to move on to other duties, but he stated, with some resignation, 'I suppose I'll have to stay and guard you, then.'

The team were relaxing and several of them were anxious to be done with their 'corpse'. One or two tried to break the discipline of the acting casualty by uncovering the face and flashing torches and shaking the 'body'. It was with some relief that I heard the end of the exercise announced.

I was 'dead' but some of my discomforts are shared by living beings, as also some of the comforts I received. It is a help to avoid vibration of the floor near the casualty, to avoid shining bright lights in the eyes, to wipe the face with a moist rag, to cover the face to keep out dust and to wrap blankets well round feet, ankles and shoulders. I learnt a lot from being 'dead'.

23

From an Exercise in *The North* — *Realism Hits Back*

I was given a briefing which I read with great interest and amusement. I was to be a street drab who would act as a look-out for two men who were to break into a shed in a builder's yard to pinch lead piping. My colleagues shared the joke and said I looked the part already, in fact they had always thought so! During the making-up and rehearsal we really worked quite a lot of atmosphere into our sordid acquaintanceship. Obviously we had met in a pub and had fixed up this break-in on the way back from the local fairground. By the time we were ready to go on the set I was beginning to enjoy being the abandoned hussy and had sharpened my down-town accent to be in keeping with my sluttish appearance.

The briefing ran that I was standing outside the shed where my associates were searching, to keep *cave* for them, when there was a crash inside, indicating that some heavy material had slipped and to be a signal for approaching first-aid teams. One of the men was badly hurt and trapped by some fallen tram rails, and the other had been knocked out by a dislodged drain pipe. My part was to act the great fright and shock caused by our predicament and this I proceeded to do as the police arrived on the scene. I could not run away so I crawled to the back of the shed and hid behind a pile of scrap metal until I was discovered.

It was a long time before the police found me and I

became much colder and very dirty. While I waited my hand came upon a small piece of paper among the dust and debris on the ground. In the dim light reaching me in my hide-out I whiled away the time by reading it. It turned out to be part of a page torn from the *Book of Common Prayer* and it said, 'Ye that do truly and earnestly repent you of your sins, and are in love and charity with your neighbours, and intend to lead a new life . . .'

Then they found me and I quickly tucked it inside my blouse, vehemently denying all knowledge of my erstwhile associates, and slumped off in the arms of the law.

But I still have the paper!

Another event showed that whether you believe it or not there are limits even for us.

It is not easy to borrow a scythe in a large city so we approached a helpful friend, a corporation official. He managed to procure one and said he got it from the crematorium. We presume it belonged to Old Father Time. We also needed some ashes with which to smother a 'casualty' in a Civil Defence incident, but perish the thought . . .!!

HELEN M. NICHOLSON

24

We Acquire a New President

Presidents Glyn Hughes and St J.D. Buxton

Brigadier H. L. Glyn Hughes, C.B.E., D.S.O., M.C., M.R.C.S., L.R.C.P., Q.H.P., became our president at the beginning of 1953. He was at that time medical director of the North West Metropolitan Regional Hospital Board and busy man that he was he had no hesitation in accepting the office we had offered him and which he was to serve generously for many years. It was perhaps a critical time because the value of our activities were beginning to be recognized.

Her Royal Highness the Princess Royal spoke of the great value of trained 'casualties' at the presentation the Stanley Shields after the Red Cross first aid and nursing competitions held in the Friends' Meeting House and the Countess of Limerick thanked the union for its assistance in the final and eliminating rounds of the contest. Later when visiting Cornwall H.R.H. referred to the importance of 'casualties'. The *West Briton and Royal Cornwall Gazette* reported that H.R.H. spoke 'pointing out that the Red Cross in Cornwall co-operated with Casualties Union who provided patients, and that she was sure that this had been a great benefit to both parties.' This was perhaps the third royal mention of Casualties Union and all members were proud of the approbation which it indicated.

Reference was made to the work of the union at that time in the 'Call of St. John in South Africa'. An article headed 'Casualties Union' commenced by stating, 'Although it has no connection with the Order of St. John, we feel that something must be said for that very live band of first aiders, the Cape Town branch of Casualties Union.' The article went on to detail the 'casualties' and 'accidents' that the branch had produced to assist St. John, Red Cross, Scouts, Railways, etc., and ended, 'We salute this hard working band of first aiders who are doing so much to promote the Order's work of First Aid.' This was most encouraging because although it continued to confuse the union with a first aid organization it showed that the work of the branch was really appreciated.

25

Eric Claxton Visits Groups and Branches in The Midlands and South West of England

A pedestrian guiding a car out of a driveway,
knocks a cyclist off her machine

I said I was both honoured and thrilled by the warmth of welcome extended to me by officers and members of St. John, Red Cross, Civil Defence and industry as well as by members of the union and their medical advisers. The spirit in which our members set about their tasks was an inspiration to me as well as to many others who witnessed the work or indeed worked with them.

I heard tales of their work which made me very proud of the standard the union had set. I saw several 'casualties' who had been so good that nobody would have had doubts as to the 'accidents' being genuine. One girl who had a large piece of a delicious looking apple wedged in her throat gave me an awful shock and I was greatly relieved when an expert first aider from the audience dashed forward and with some difficulty removed the obstruction. I saw a brilliant nose-bleed, and I saw a girl who had grazed her wrist when the lever on a motor plough was inadvertently tripped.

A nasty scald occurred during what was otherwise a most pleasant picnic under the trees in a shady garden. I also reported meeting some enthusiasts who had the misfortune to meet with a motor cycle 'accident' in the middle of the street in the rain and one of the 'casualties' had been knocked down and was lying in the wet and dirty street.

This last group were heart-broken because I didn't find sufficient faults. 'We learn from our faults once we know what they are,' they told me. What a grand spirit.

On my return I said, 'I was also very impressed by the understanding and enthusiasm of the medical advisers whom I met. Their guidance and criticism is so important to the development and maintenance of our standard. I want them to know how much we value and appreciate the grand job they are doing with us. I want to say this, not only to the doctors whom I met, but to our medical advisers in other places who are doing a similar job with the same enthusiasm. May I also say to other doctors who may chance to read these notes that we should greatly value their support too, if they can spare a little time to advise us and to give us the benefit of their experience by criticising our work. Unless our work is good it is not good enough.'

26

Blood Transfusion

No doubt all our members, and in fact all our readers of the journal too, would have been interested in the demonstration of a blood transfusion illustrated in the tenth anniversary issue. Because every member learned to portray the signs and symptoms of shock and their progress both up and down, we were greatly impressed by the remarkable effect of blood or plasma transfusion. Therefore no section of the community could be more aware of the ever present need of blood donors. I appealed to readers of the journal to consider whether they could themselves become blood donors. It is quite painless; it presents so little inconvenience and, such as it does, takes the form of half an hour's rest with a cup of tea and some biscuits. Time — almost at your own convenience — at lunch time, on the way home or in the slack times of the day. It is surprising how little inconvenience this gift involves, yet it may nevertheless be the means of ensuring someone else's life, health and happiness. It can become an occasion to look forward to three times each year. The team of doctors and nurses who run this service are among the most charming, kind and efficient people one could ever meet. Let us back them up, because they will never let us down.

27

Tenth Anniversary Celebration Dinner

This had been postponed for a year due to the sudden
death of our former president Major-General P. H.
Mitchener. Brigadier Glyn Hughes was able to set in train a
new plan for the postponed dinner at the Royal College of
Surgeons. A symposium of commentaries was prepared by
several grades of members.

How can one convey to those of our members who
were not able to be there the magic of the
occasion? It was indeed a delightful and a happy
occasion. From the moment one set foot inside the
Royal College building, one felt a warm atmosphere and a perfect evening had begun.

The buildings were undergoing extension involving the central staircase, but in spite of this the
central hall provided a suitable spot for the
reception by the president and Mrs Glyn Hughes,
who performed the honour with grace and
distinction. There was a pleasant chatter as guests
and members mingled, having drinks and finding
their places on the seating plan. As the name of
each newcomer was announced groups broke and
joined again and the latest arrival had been
drawn into the harmony of the whole.

The welcome sound of, *Mr President, Ladies and
Gentlemen — dinner is served,*' started a procession

upstairs to the library. There the table stretched the full length of the room with six spurs. It looked beautiful with its gleaming silver and glass, and the brilliant red carnations upon the white linen, contrasting with the background of leather-bound volumes round the walls and gallery banked with more and more books overhead. A perfect setting.

The company of seventy-five settled down to a simple but excellent dinner of mushroom soup, whitebait, turkey and ice cream, suitably balanced by delightful wines.

Dinner was followed by a series of speeches and five toasts were drunk. The least that could be said of the speeches was that they were brief but adequate. There were no epics of oratory but each one contributed to that feeling of harmony which had been experienced earlier. Here was indeed a group of friends forgathered to celebrate an important event. Our guests acknowledged the work the union had done and expressed in no uncertain terms their sincere wish that Casualties Union should go from strength to strength in the second ten years.

The toasts were simple and in order. Firstly, 'Her Majesty.' Secondly, 'The First Aid Societies,' *the end* which we all serve, which must come next. Thirdly 'Casualties Union,' which provides *living training equipment* for the first aid and rescue organizations to use as a means to *the end*. Fourthly, 'Our guests,' distinguished in the fields of surgery and medicine or responsible for the shock troops who take the brunt of the attack in peace and wartime disaster. And lastly, but by no manner of means least, 'The President.' Some of us had a private thought at that moment of that other great man, who would so much have enjoyed presiding at our gathering, and whose influence had gained for us the invitation to the Royal College, Major-General P. H. Mitchiner, whose untimely death had caused the dinner to be postponed. It was, however, a happy memory and our thoughts returned with growing affection to his successor, Dr Glyn Hughes, and to Mrs Hughes who had graced the proceedings with her charming presence.

A SENIOR OFFICER

During dinner, and between toasts and speeches, which will be commented on by others, I had an opportunity to study our surroundings. There we were, probably the newest and youngest offshoot of a very great and ancient profession, surrounded by many thousands of books ranging over the developments in the arts of healing right back to the beginning of our civilization to the latest discoveries of our present age. It would indeed be wonderful if one day the work of Casualties Union should fine a niche in that Hall of Great Knowledge.

A FOUNDER MEMBER

From the moment of entering the famous portals of the Royal College of Surgeons to be charmingly received by our president and his wife, the occasion of the tenth anniversary dinner was a thoroughly happy and informal affair. The spirit of friendliness and enthusiasm between officials and members and the eagerness and generosity with which ideas and experiences were pooled, made an outstanding impression, I am sure, on all who were fortunate enough to be present. By arranging the seating at the dinner tables so that members did not sit beside those they knew best, the maximum degree of interest and discussion was ensured.

The presence of so many distinguished guests representing Medicine and Surgery, the Forces, the Home Office, the First Aid Societies, Industry and the Press, encouraged us all in the realisation that widespread notice was being taken in our activities. I feel sure that from the understanding nature of the speeches our guests went away determined and willing to use their influence in furthering the object of Casualties Union, which is to help first-aiders to deal humanely with injured people.

I returned to my hotel thrilled to be a pioneer member of such a worthwhile movement.

A NEW MEMBER

The President, Dr. H. L. Glyn Hughes, C.B.E., D.S.O., M.C., M.R.C.S., L.R.C.P., Q.H.P., in the chair.

TOASTS

'Her Majesty the Queen'

'The First Aid Societies'

Proposed by F. H. Lowe Esq., *Honorary Member.*
Response by Air Commodore H. A. Hewat,
C.B.E., M.D., *Medical Adviser,*
British Red Cross Society.
Followed by Brigadier T. D. Daly, C.B.E., M.C.,
Deputy Commissioner in Chief,
St. John Ambulance Brigade.

'The Union — the Second Ten Years'

Proposed by Colonel T. Woods, O.B.E., M.D.,
Commandant, Depot and
Training Establishment, R.A.M.C.
Seconded by Dr. John Rogan, M.D., *Chief*
Medical Officer, National Coal Board.
Response by E. C. Claxton, M.B.E., B.Sc.,
A.M.I.C.E., A.F.I.C.D.,
Chairman of Council.

'Our Guests'

Proposed by the President.
Response by Sir Heneage Ogilvie, K.C.B.,
M.C., F.R.C.S.,
Followed by Sir Earnest Rock Carling, F.R.C.S.,
F.R.C.P., *Adviser to the Home Office*

'The President'

Proposed by Major-General L. A. Hawes, C.B.E.,
D.S.O., M.C., B.A. *Vice President of Casualties
Union*
Response by The President.

☆　　☆　　☆

We were also honoured to have as our guests:

Mr. John Bunyan, *Consulting Surgeon.*
Mr. F. G. Thomas, M.A., *Secretary,
National Dock Labour Board.*
Group Captain R. C. Dawkins, C.B.E.,
Commanding Officer, Royal Air Force, Hendon
Major-General W. R. Dimond, C.I.E.,
C.B.E., T.M.S.(R.), *Ministry of Health.*
Mr. R. M. North, *Civil Defence, Home
Office.*
Mr. C. S. McLeod, *Regional Staff Officer,
Eastern Region, British Railways.*
Major-General S. F. Irwin, C.B., C.B.E.,
*Chairman of Defence Committee,
Civil Defence Dept., Home Office.*
Wing Commander S. Paul, *Principal Medical
Officer, Transport Command,
Royal Air Force.*
Mr. Dale Robinson, *Editor, 'First Aid and
Nursing'.*

28

*Casualties Union Day 1953
at Royal Air Force, Hendon*

What a contrast from the previous year when our venue
had been a building site in the heart of London. When one
thinks in terms of a first aid competition, an airfield is a vast
place. However it was on the comparatively small area in
front of the control tower and hangars that the competition
was held.

As we approached the competition area we could see five
aircraft drawn up on the tarmac and beside each one an
incident had happened with which the competing teams
were dealing. The story was that a private aircraft had
flown in and a friend, in his eagerness to greet the pilot,
had been caught by the wing in the back of the neck as the
plane swung round to a standstill. While this casualty had a
fracture-dislocation of the cervical region of the spine, the
pilot had fallen while alighting and his fiancee became
scared as she ran from the control tower, but she could be
helpful if she was given a sensible job to do.

The tenseness of the spectators' faces showed not merely
that they were interested in the teams they supported, and
there were thirty-five of them, but that they were restive in
their eagerness to be allowed to handle the situation
themselves.

Near to the hangars sixteen 'casualties' had met with
accidents or had been taken suddenly ill, and pairs of
competitors were eagerly examining them and writing down

their findings at the little tables set near each case. The injuries were all carefully related to the natural setting or the equipment lent us by the R.A.F.

When the show was in full swing our guests of honour arrived; Air Marshall Sir James Kilpatrick, Director General of Medical Services, Royal Air Force, and Lady Kilpatrick, who studied the cases with great care and spoke highly of the acting and the realism with which the sixteen conditions listed below were staged:

Rigor, onset of malaria; severe dog bite of right arm; rupture of liver; closed fracture of tibia; severed extensor tendon, ring finger; burns from CO fire extinguisher; diabetic collapse, gangrene of great toe; barbiturate poisoning; air sickness; oxygen burns; electric shock with lacerated leg; wound of temple; depressed fracture of malar; overcome by dope fumes and dislocated shoulder; severed flexor tendon, left index finger; closed fracture ribs.

The R.A.M.C. Visual Aid Team and the R.A.F. Medical Services both staged demonstrations of the use they made of trained casualties in active service conditions.

Inside one of the large hangars were displays of the Royal Society for the Prevention of Accidents and the Institute of Civil Defence, both colourful and very instructive. Our own Study Circle corner and Information Bureau drew crowds of visitors. At intervals a string of five R.A.F. ambulances would come tearing across the airfield, ringing their bells wildly, bringing competing teams to the scene of action. Very thrilling!

As dusk began to fall we gathered on the tarmac to hear the president's remarks and the results, and to watch the guest of honour presenting the awards. It had been remarked that over the period of ten years our trophies had been won five times each by Red Cross and St. John. To keep the balance on this happy occasion, we were pleased to present them this year to a team from industry who won top marks in each section. We parted hoping to meet everyone again next year.

But as always the packing up had still to be done; when this was almost completed, the commanding Officer sent me a message to meet him in the Officers' Mess. Over a drink the C.O. reminded me of their arrangement, made at the time of his agreeing to the union being guests at Hendon, that there should be a retiring collection by the R.A.F. personnel for some Air Force charity. That satisfactory collection had now been handed to him as agreed, but he felt that Casualties Union could make even greater use of the money and passed it over to me.

Hospitality at its most generous and helpful in every way! Thanks R.A.F.

29

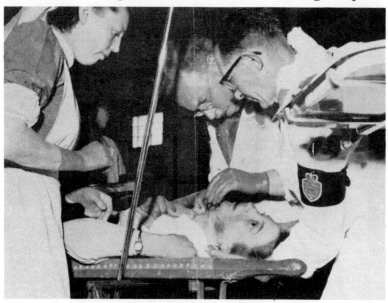

An emergency tracheotomy

The Minister of Health, Mr. Iain Macleod, watched sixteen mobile first aid teams compete for the final honours in the competition for the most efficient unit in the Metropolitan Hospital Regions on the Horse Guards Parade on 19th September, 1953. The challenge cup presented by the Minister of Health was won by the Enfield Hospital Group.

Four competition sets were in action simultaneously. In

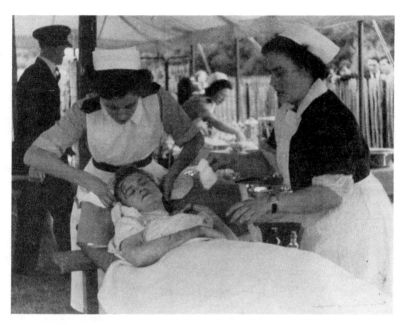
Nurses treating a trained casualty at Ascot Racecourse

order to maintain the continuous supply of 'casualties' and to ensure that the make-up was always fresh for each team, over forty members took part. We felt that it was a privilege to give this service, and we were very pleased that the Minister of Health and Mrs. Macleod showed such interest in the production of 'casualties' by spending some time in the make-up tent. The cases provided on each set were an open fracture of the tibia, a compound fracture and a depressed fracture of the skull, simple fracture of the middle shaft of humerus, sprained ankle and abrasions to face and knees.

The Ministry of Health hoped that the following year the competition could be run on a national basis with all fourteen hospital regions taking part. The union hoped to be able to meet all the commitments that arose from such a decision to expand nationwide.

30

Study Circles Justify Their Foundation

The Journal for November, 1953 reported: The autumn boom in Study Circles has brought probationers to our calling all over the country. We welcome them all and wish them success in the great adventure of training as 'casualties'. Since the summer break new Study Circles were started at:

> Newbury S.C. 174. B.R.C.S.;
> Kensington S.C. 175. B.R.C.S.;
> Teddington S.C. 193. Industry;
> Cowdenbeath S.C. 194. N.C.B.;
> Dawlish S.C. 195. B.R.C.S.;
> Sheringham S.C. 196. B.R.C.S.;
> Malton, Yorks. S.C. 197. B.R.C.S.;
> Barnet, Herts. S.C. 198. B.R.C.S.;
> Chorley, Lancs. S.C. 199. C.D.;
> Slough, Bucks. (now Berks.) S.C. 200. S.J.A.B.

Under the title 'The Importance of Being Earnest' we received the following article from Mr. H. Coleman, leader of Liverpool Street S.C. 152. British Railways.

'The dictionary gives the meaning of the word "earnest" as being, briefly, "sincere or serious," and I wish to consider the phrase from a Casualties Union viewpoint. Our endeavour is to depict certain injuries or reactions to the best of our ability in such a way as to give the onlooker the impression that one is actually suffering from the injuries in question. To do this, it is necessary for the casualty to become attuned to the circumstances or history of the case. In other words, he must understand exactly what has happened and how it happened. He must then try to appreciate both in mind and body the surprise, shock and pain which is to be expected, and the extent of the injury or injuries assumed.

'Take the mental reaction: one must try to visualize the case, the anxiety, the apprehension and fear to a major or minor degree which will be experienced in an actual case. Then there is the resultant degree of shock arising from the mental state. How could one possibly depict this without a desire to put over the case correctly?

'Again there is the bodily reaction to the result of the accident — in other words, the reaction to the injury. How will one respond immediately? Can one move without more pain? Is there any blood? Will it upset the patient further and so cause greater shock? What about danger and possibility of additional injuries by staying put? All these points must be fully appreciated by the patient to enable him to act the part. He could not do this without a real desire to know as much as possible about the case.

'Then the casualty must be able to imitate or *ACT*, and this requires special training in order to make the muscles of the body behave *at will* in a similar way as would be the case in our involuntary response to injury. To assist in the acting, one creates a reproduction of the injury, commonly called "faking", and here again another side of the casualty is opened up. His ability to reproduce realistically the cuts, burns, swelling and fractures helps to make the picture. All this cannot be done without long practice and the wish to illustrate, true to form, an incident. It really goes beyond the wish; it becomes an *earnest desire,* and I think the points mentioned will emphasise in no uncertain terms the Importance of Being Earnest.'

☆　　☆　　☆

Another delightful contribution reached us from a Cheshire Study Circle.

CUCU

*(With acknowledgement and apologies to John Keats
and his Nightingale)*

My heart aches and a drowsy numbness pains
    My sense, as though of hemlock I had drunk,
My pulse is slow, my feet in leaden chains,
    My face is pale, my head on bosom sunk.
Why sit I here, both friendless and alone
    When I could laughing with my fellows be?
I am beside myself — another grown —
    Poor hapless wretch! I am a Casualty.

Far, far away, dissolve and quite forget
    All inhibitions I have ever known,
Prepare to act the fever and the fret
    And sit and hear each other groan.
Not for a beaker full of the warm south
    But liquid blood of natural hue I ask.
For cuts and wounds and lacerated mouth.
    A Vampire? Nay, a Casualty's my task!

Sometimes I try like Alchemist of old
    To mix my fearful potions and make brews
For filling blisters. Plastercine I mould,
    To match the different skins, the colours, chose,
Capsules I suck 'til beaded bubbles wink,
    Upon the rim of frothy blood-stained lips
Beneath these heavy burdens do I sink?
    No, Casualties Union gives the latest tips.

As birds in autumn to some southern clime
    I and my fellow CUCUS do depart
To London. there in Bedford College grand
    To meet our friends, past-masters of their art,
Our modest contribution there to show,
    Discuss with them our problems large and small,
How shall our Circles widen yet and grow,
    'Til casualties can answer every call?

Then later when the evening shadows fall,
    We meet again in party plumage bright
Within the surgeon's Royal College Hall,
    Spread are the tables with fair damask white,
With richly gleaming silver, glass and flowers
    A banquet fit for Kings. Many a toast
Is drunk and witty speech beguiles the hours,
    And all in C.U. gossip are engrossed.

To Hendon Airfield for the Final Day,
    Where casualties around the damaged 'planes
Are laid, and first aid teams to all display
    How best they can alleviate their pains.
Then are they called upon to diagnose,
    All aches and pains to which the flesh is heir,
At last when all are surfeited with woes
    To see who's gained the prizes we repair.

Homeward the tired, but happy CUCUS fly,
    In winged chariots through the starry night,
The darkling towns and villages rush by,
    And Lichfield's trinity of towers so bright.
Was it a vision or a waking dream —
    Now much refreshed we're all back home again
Determined that our Casualties Union Team
    Shall work until the highest skills attain.

D. JAMES,
Altrincham Study Circle.

3I

Members Research

It certainly is not all fun. Southend-on-Sea Study Circle offered this advice on blood pumps. The apparatus can be built up from the following components:

(A). Blood reservoir. Eight inch length of motor-cycle inner tube (including valve stem), sealed both ends by vulcanising at a tyre depot. This reservoir is sewn onto a flannel cover with tapes attached to corners.

(B). Rubber bulb of Higginson's syringe with one-way valve at (C).

(D). Rubber suction tube, ¼ ins. int. dia.

(E). U-bend made by water heating vulcanite tube from Higginson's set.

(F). 'Artery' consisting of suitable length of windscreen-wiper tube.

(G). Spring clip.

It is assembled as follows:

A suitable wound is prepared over the artery assumed to be injured and the end of the rubber 'artery' (F) is buried in the heart side of the wound. Care must be taken to keep the end of artery clear of putty, etc. The jet should be directed more across the wound than outwards to reduce damage to clothes of F.A. team.

The 'artery' is attached to the patient's skin at intervals by means of strapping and then its other end connected to outlet of bulb (B) which is held in the patient's hand (one upper limb should be kept free from 'injury' for this purpose).

As the bulb is held in the palm of the hand the U-tube hangs downward so that the suction tube (D) returns up the same arm to be connected to reservoir which is carried below the armpit on the same side, and attached to the trunk and neck by means of tapes.

Before connecting reservoir a clip should be placed to seal the 'artery' as near to the wound as possible. Blood (left overs from transfusions), which should be brightened by having coal gas bubbled through it, is filled into the reservoir through a small funnel. Air should be expelled from reservoir which is then connected to the suction tube.

Test apparatus by holding a receiver at wound, releasing clip and instructing patient to pump gently. As soon as blood spurts freely, re-apply clip. Suitable mutilated clothing may now be put on over the apparatus and the patient placed in position avoiding pressure on reservoir.

The last job when the scene is set is for an assistant to release (not remove) clip. Similarly as soon as the 'curtain falls' this clip should be re-applied. The following inevitable problems can easily be solved locally, i.e. spare set for relief patient, protection of floor surface, 'handling damage' to patient's wound, patient's 'pumping' reaction when pressure correctly applied.

32

Hughie Glyn Hughes, Our President,
Takes Us Into Another Year

To all members of Casualties Union, both personally and collectively, I would like to wish a very happy and prospering New Year in 1954.

It is just twelve months since I was elected your president, and during this time I do feel I have got to know many of you well and realize and appreciate what valuable work the union is doing. I would like to stress here and now that I am quite sure the scope of our work will, in the near future, be increased very considerably: Civil Defence with its ever increasing requirements in the way of training, exercises and demonstrations will make demands upon us and we must make every effort to increase our members so that we can meet these commitments and any others that may be placed upon us. I am quite confident that with the wonderful esprit de corps which exists throughout the union your efforts will succeed.

The record of your work during the past year makes very impressive reading and the number of 'activities' carried out by some Study Circles is amazing. When I attend exercises in which members are taking part I always feel so very proud of the efficient performance that is put up and never can resist basking in 'reflected glory'. I am quite sure also that many more of those responsible for the training of the first aid and casualty services of the country will realize the help that can be given to them; from my own knowledge I do know that your efforts are being more and more widely appreciated.

Study Circles are growing in number and to all those newly formed I send my best wishes and hope that at some future date I may be able to visit them. The year that is past has been a memorable one in the celebration of our tenth anniversary, and I look forward to the next ten years with every confidence and hope that we shall proceed from strength to strength.

I would like to leave you just one thought in this New Year; it is taken from the Objects of your Constitution which express so very well the ideals for which you work. I refer to your aim to disseminate the knowledge you have gained for the benefit of humanity and to devote all your efforts without thought of personal benefit. What better goal can we aim at.

Good luck and good wishes to you all.

GLYN HUGHES, 1954

33

Commentary 1954

At last in writing these notes I have the pleasure and privilege of being able to address every member and probationer member of the union, as well as a large number of senior officers of the medical, health and rescue services and other friends of the union. I hope that they will find much in common. We have at least to face the brutal fact that a thousand persons a day are injured on the roads and in the factories of this country. A fact that shows the urgent need for trained first aid and rescue personnel in peacetime as well as in war.

The voluntary aid societies and Civil Defence exist to teach first aid and rescue work, and the union exists to help them by training personnel to portray as faithfully as may be possible the behaviour of injured persons, so that the students may be given practical experience in handling 'wounded' and 'dying' in situations which first-aiders are constantly called upon to face. This practical work not only makes training more interesting but it gives the opportunity for making first-aid diagnosis, and determining and applying treatment on the spot, extricating the injured person from the situation and providing transport. It also provides practice for the mobile first aid posts and nursing services.

I hope that my readers will be disposed to help the union in two ways:

● If you are a member of the union will you become a

Cucury demonstration to sell the journal

subscriber to this journal? The cost is trifling (2/6 per annum for four issues), but we need a much greater circulation to justify the drastic reduction in price from 7/6 per annum. You may care to use the loose form inserted in this issue, or persuade a friend to do so.

● Send us your constructive criticism of this journal, of the work of the union, of the union itself.

We do appreciate the constructive criticism which our friends give us — both new friends and old. I think it is perhaps a special quality of our membership that we can take constructive criticism — and that is a good thing for it is the only way we can hope to reach the standard we have set out to achieve. Unless the behaviour of an 'injured' person is *good enough* to cause a doctor to hesitate, to look a second time just in case, then the 'casualty' is just *not good enough*.

A large part of the union's efforts are devoted to assisting St. John and Red Cross. Their demands are remarkably equal, and across the border we find our members able also to help St. Andrew. Although an entirely voluntary organisation, we have been able to give a considerable amount of assistance to the police, to the medical units of the fighting services and also to industrial concerns. We are proud of these associations — with the coal industry in nearly every coalfield, with dockworkers and railwaymen, postal and fire services and, of course, the growing demands of Civil Defence throughout the country.

Recently I had the pleasure of addressing a gathering of Civil Defence officers of Government Departments in Treasury Chambers. Brenda Whiteley, Nancy Budgett and Cyril Wallace gave a series of demonstrations and the spectators began to realize the value of this method for conducting practical training and everyone present agreed that it is an insult to your part-time volunteer to invite him to undertake courses where the training is not both practical and objective. Hence for first aid and rescue, trained expert 'casualties' are essential.

Members will, I know, like to join me in offering congratulations to our president, Dr Glyn Hughes, upon his recent appointment as Honorary Physician to Her Majesty the Queen.

The union was pleased to be invited by the Home Office to provide casualties for a Civil Defence exercise at the Isle of Dogs in the Thames off Greenwich. The casualties after rescue, were transported by ferry boat for hospital treatment. The situation was created as a test for the experimental mobile column, the Civil Defence Corps and the N.H.S.R. We have helped to provide many tests for the mobile column in many parts of the country but this was the first occasion when they have been called upon to transport their 'casualties' by water.

Another interesting development has been the National Dock Labour Board's weekend school at Beatrice Webb House on the side of Leith Hill in Surrey. The union provided casualties for demonstration, diagnosis and treatment, and also provided an 'accident' for a practice team test in a friendly competition. The enthusiastic reception of our members' assistance by the students, lecturing doctors and judges was most encouraging.

During the past year the union has managed to render more assistance than ever before, over two events a day on

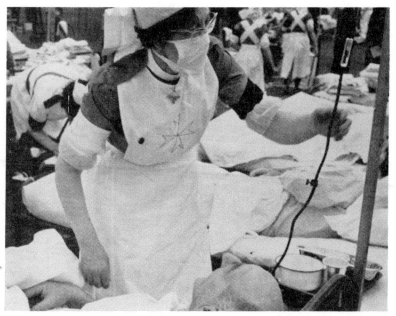
Working with N.H.S.R. in Autumn 1961

average throughout the year. The demand by the First Aid societies, Civil Defence, National Hospital Service Reserve and others continue to increase substantially each year, and we need more trained members to help us to maintain our record of ever ready willingness to help anywhere. Enthusiasts who are willing to gather together in groups can be trained in Study Circles. Individuals who are near to existing branches may be able to train with them. There is no gainsaying it's a very fascinating study and one experiences a side of first-aid which is both instructive and interesting. It is also very well worth-while.

ERIC CLAXTON

34

The Teaching of Acting —
'On Being Beside Oneself'

In response to many requests from Study Circles for help in the teaching of acting, I am going to try to convince you that we hardly need to be taught acting at all, because we are all acting all day long. What needs to be done is to draw out and make full use of our natural abilities.

> The little actor cons another part
> Filling from time to time his humerous stage
> With all the persons, down to palsied Age,
> That life brings with her in equipage.
> As if his whole vocation
> Were endless imitation.

'Endless imitation.' Some people wax rather reproachful if you suggest to them that we are all actors in our daily lives, even in our most intimate relationships, that we quickly assume one role, then another, adapting our performance to suit our audience. We are indeed 'all things to all men.'

Ask yourself how many 'I's' there are in acting. Only one if you are a good speller, but many if you follow my argument that we are all compounded of a number of 'I's' which together make up the personality by which we are known. Submit the 'self' of which we speak to even a superficial analysis, or some kind of shock, some disconcerting experience — the death of a person on whom one

Conference at Nottingham

depends, a motor smash, or a disturbing emotional upheaval, and we may well find ourselves asking at such a time, 'What has become of me?' or perhaps, saying afterwards, 'I did not know myself.'

I am convinced that in our study of the teaching of acting we ought to take literally the exclamation, 'I am beside myself!' Let us practice mentally the exercise of being beside ourselves. Stand outside of yourself and look objectively at the self which is you at any given moment. A most revealing experience.

Watch yourself meeting someone for the first time — someone on whom you wish to make a good impression. You are asking yourself, 'Which of my various roles shall I play in order to impress this person?' You can almost hear the pressing of buttons, the throwing of levers, the preening and tail-wagging which are involved in the process of personal relationships. We do this not only with out minds but with our bodies as well. The mental pattern produces the correct expressions, the gestures, the words and the physical bearing related to the situation.

I believe we can cultivate this method of 'being beside oneself' and in it we shall find much of the solution to the problem of self-consciousness. I am sure that it is an obstinate refusal to come out of the 'self' which we believe binds us to reality, that causes us to indulge in an extravagant orgy of 'nerves' when we are required to make a speech or act as a casualty. If, as I am supposing, we are all commonly playing the part of many different selves all day long, it must be possible to adapt our ability to play the injured self with equal conviction. Staging can be taught, make-up can be demonstrated, but acting can only be drawn out. No amount of my acting it for you, will produce a similar performance on your part. Each student must make the situation his, or her own, and all an instructor can do is develop by drawing out, the natural ability to bring the whole being into line with any given injuries and situations.

How can this be done? Play it first of all. Get past the funny stage in the very early part of probationer training. Then try a few games to break the ice and to establish a drill which will open up fascinating possibilities of creating situations with simple examples of the use of gesture and voice inflection to express emotion, pain, anxiety and confidence.

Practise controlling the facial expression by playing the old party game, 'Throwing the smile.' Do you remember it from your childhood days? One member of the party has a broad grin which he wipes off and throws to the next person who can have a good laugh until she passes the grin round the circle. All but the one with the smile must behave very solemnly. A really sound approach to acting and good training in concentration.

In a small group of about six members study the different expressions assumed by the eyes, mouth and hands to express weariness, happiness, anxiety and pain. Study each feature separately with its mental background. some expressions indicate a complete change of bodily tone as in a case of shock where every feature falls into line with that condition. The happy person becomes 'beside herself' by altering the whole mental background of her expression.

You can change in character as well as in condition. This is done partly with make-up, but the mental background must be there too. Unless you have *made up your mind,* grease paint cannot help you.

Another game that will help you in developing acting ability needs only a title to make it popular at parties. Make a list of short phrases such as these:

'Mind what you're doing!'
'Let me tell you.'
'It came from above.'
'Where is she now?'
'Oh! It's gone!'
'I can't see anything.'
'I was coming downstairs.'

And taking each phrase in turn let each player say it differently, using it to express several emotions and situations by changing inflection, while the others guess in what circumstances it would be said in each particular way. You will be astonished at the hidden resources of the histrionic art which your students will reveal to themselves and you will find that they have learned quite a lot without having to teach them anything.

MRS. HELEN M. NICHOLSON, *Senior Instructor.*

35

Problems of Teaching Casualties Union Technique

From the medical adviser's point of view the problems of teaching Casualties Union technique may be conveniently divided into three sets:

- Problems associated with the art of faking wounds, injuries and medical or associated conditions.
- Problems associated with the art of acting the part of the wounded or injured person.
- Administrative or teaching problems.

The art of faking

Casualties Union technique in its highest form can produce something very like the real thing, but imitation must be an accurate copy of the real thing. Therefore, it is essential for all members to see as many real injuries as possible, and by constant revision, to keep the actual appearance of wounds, compound fractures, new or old bruises and other medico-surgical conditions fresh in their minds. Too often there is a tendency to rely on the memory for details of a wound or injury, so that the member produces 'what I think a compound fracture looks like,' or worse still, 'what I think it *ought* to look like.' Memories are apt to be rather volatile and hazy; the passage of time erases details and the general impression becomes blurred. For this reason it is desirable that Casualties Union members should see a reasonable number of actual injury cases in a given period of time. So make sure that all your members are practising members of at least one voluntary first aid movement, for by this method they will stand a better chance of seeing and treating real injuries. You cannot hope to copy anything unless you look at the original closely and often.

Even when members are fulfilling these conditions it is still a great problem to maintain a sense of proportion; at first the make-up colours tend to be too bright and startling, the patch of plasticine too obviously stuck on the skin, and much too much blood is spilled around. This, I find, is one of the biggest problems facing the medical adviser; just how to maintain the sense of proportion. Most members in their early days are very liberal with their use of the blood mixture, but in time they learn to restrain themselves and put on the right amount. A few, it must be admitted, persist with liberal applications of blood well into their maturity.

This is one of the reasons why I consider that Casualties Union work and first aid training should go hand in hand. One can only acquire knowledge of the natural state of affairs by seeing actual injuries. You may think that severe lacerations cause a great loss of blood; possibly some do, but shock very rapidly lowers the blood pressure so that bleeding decreases proportionately.

Don't wallow in a blood bath. Your casualties can be most dramatic with only a few ounces of blood, which all things considered, including the economic side, is quite enough to stain the floor and clothing, and may well be rather more than the average blood loss. Gunshot wounds, war wounds and severe road injuries on the other hand may need to be overdone purposely in order to drive home a lesson in first aid.

Aids to faking of injuries and the use of illustrations

(A) By the collection of pictures from surgical or medical text books, from the trade literature of the numerous drug houses and manufacturing chemists (a prolific source of illustrated leaflets), from medico-legal text books (i.e.,

Glaister, a Text Book of Medical Jurisprudence) and from popular magazines (i.e., *Family Doctor)* and first aid magazines: from all these impressions of particular wounds or injuries may be obtained.

(B) By the study of x-ray films (to see positions of bones in normal and abnormal states), medical drawings (most big hospitals have full time medical illustrators, who are usually most helpful), and possible case notes of actual injuries. This last point may present some difficulty, but copies of the *Lancet* or *British Medical Journal* are readily obtainable and contain case histories of unusual injuries or interesting conditions from time to time.

(C) The use of own members' notes and drawings. this could be a very useful source of information if fully developed: members should be encouraged to write descriptions of actual injuries observed by them and if possible illustrate them. By this means the experience of one person is made available to several others.

The art of acting

The art of acting, as I understand it, consists in getting under the skin of the part to be played and staying there, fusing one's own personality into that of the created person. And this is precisely what you must do when you play the part of an injured person, a person not merely injured in body and limbs, but mentally shocked and injured in mind as well. It is necessary to understand the psychology of the injured person and to realize two things: one, that the last thing he expected was bodily harm to come to him; and two, the fact that no two persons react in the same way to a particular injury. You must study these variations and select the right reactions for the part you have to play.

Plan for teaching

My limited experience in the realm of Casualties Union has taught me a number of points.

It is essential to have a plan or programme for teaching.

Let your members know in advance what the subjects for the next meeting will be. Do not drift aimlessly along otherwise you will lose your class members. Have a programme and stick to it, and have an alternative plan up your sleeve, in case you have to make a change. Practice in class must be reinforced by practice at home. It is essential for novices to learn to accept criticism from all and sundry.

I am a great believer in the 'class' method of teaching Casualties Union technique, particularly in the more difficult matters of fainting, throwing fits or breathing stertorously. These medical phenomena should be portrayed correctly, and should be performed under the direct supervision of the medical adviser.

Learning Casualties Union technique is absorbing, but one can become bogged down in a deadly routine with the greatest of ease. Therefore keep the interest of your members stimulated. Have a discussion from time to time or produce some unusual injury for the consideration of the class or set a problem for individual members to work out. Discussions set people talking and new ideas must then evolve.

Periodic testing

It is desirable to organize a series of tests throughout the training period and to institute a system of marking. The first tests should be carried out after fair warning but, as the members become more experienced, the warning period can be shortened.

Testing proves that advice is being accepted and followed, progress is being made and the class is acquiring confidence in itself.

Natural approach

Finally, I would make one plea for a natural approach to injuries and accidents. There is, I think, too great a tendency in our midst to select an injury and then build up an accident or incident around it. Teach your members to select an accident and then to *work out what would be the most likely set of injuries:* in fact, you must study the mechanics of moving vehicles or falling bodies of men or women in order to get the right answer.

Freak accidents apart, the average accident produces far less ill effect than the average first aid competition would suggest. This tendency to 'over injure', admittedly genuine enough in the circumstances, gives a wrong impression. Many accidents result in nothing more than a severe 'shaking up' — and that's a darling part to play!

Medical conditions and injuries cover a vast territory. So many variations may arise, so many different factors may be at work. Doctors and scientists are always learning, so also must Casualties Union members.

You have a new subject, a new technique in your hands. Go ahead and use it naturally and revise continually the great art of faking an injury and the greater art of portraying a human being, bruised in body and injured in mind. Be natural and imitate the real wounds. Then may you emulate David Garrick, the greatest actor of all time, of whom Oliver Goldsmith wrote:

'On the stage he was natural, simple, affecting;
'Twas only that when he was off he was acting.'

J. S. BINNING, M.B., Ch.B.
Medical Adviser, Study circle 152,
Liverpool Street Station (B.R.)

36

Snapshots of Some of Our
Most Hard-Working Members

In this collation of articles and reports of the milestones which Casualties Union has already set, we have told with pride of the splendid men who have been our presidents. In some of the other reports we have referred to some very hard working members who have done much to set the standard of Casualties Union achievement. These snapshots written at the time by friends and admirers give a personal picture of some of them.

DOCTOR J. E. HAINE. A very tower of strength, and the one person who has never been known to say no to any request for aid since the union's very beginning. In the early days, the Guildford Rural Civil Defence took perhaps a little unthinkingly what he gave; and it was only when we heard of other areas' difficulties with petrol, transport and make-up that we began to appreciate fully our own M.O.H. When the war was over and everyone said, 'To blazes with first-Aid! We have had enough of it!'; many members had almost decided to disband the union; but Dr. Haine said in no uncertain terms that we had no choice, that we must carry on with so vital a job and if we were not prepared to do so he would be forced to start on his own.

The calls we have made upon his time have been legion.

His staff have typed and duplicated for us, his advice on policy has influenced the union, his brain has been mercilessly picked for medical details, he has 'vetted' briefings, and played with the mechanics of many things to get results.

What is he like? Tall, erect, with dark crisp curly hair going a little grey, hazel eyes with interesting flecks in them, uses strong glasses. Usually wears very loose collars that match a shirt of perhaps apple-green or golden yellow. Used to wear a kilt, but says his wife won't let him now. Yes; he's a Scot. A more than excellent lecturer with a soft voice that is so pitched that no-one listening ever misses a word, and a quiet dry humour, usually poking fun at himself over something that has worked to his own disadvantage. As an interesting sidelight he loves driving very fast and powerful cars. Interests — gardening, golf, and (strangely enough) Casualties Union.

☆ ☆ ☆

MRS BRENDA WHITELEY. A man attempting to draw a pen portrait of a woman requires more than the average amount of tact, and a fair amount of courage. The writer is not taking any chances, but he will say this much. Our First Lady is somewhat diminutive; her charm and vivacity are all the greater. To meet her, you would scarcely credit her with more than, say, twenty-four summers (although the reverse of these figures might be nearer the mark). Her heart is warm and generous; in fact, she is a feline without the cattiness. She has a most infectious laugh. With this brief glimpse, we must pass from — shall we say — tact to fact.

Brenda Whiteley, founder member, vice-president of the union, member of the committee, senior instructor, and quartermaster, is the origin of the species, definitely the first female "casualty'. A born actress, what talent scouts would describe as a 'natural', she reigns supreme in every branch of our activities. A severe critic, but only of her own imagined shortcomings. It is difficult not to make extravagant claims for her, but to put it mildly, she has been a source of inspiration to which we owe most of our strength

Brenda Whiteley waits patiently to be buried in a
corrugated iron box under hundreds of tons of debris

and unity today.

None of the founder members will forget the early days of
the union when she would tactfully allocate parts to each of
us according to our primitive abilities, invariably choosing
witbout hesitation the foulest, most dangerous and uncomfortable job for herself. Nor again, at a much later date,
when a 'drowned' body was required in the canal at
Guildford on the coldest winter day imaginable, was there
even any discussion as to who would undertake the task.
Brenda it was.

She is at present, to use her own words, 'taking a little
rest,' but until her recent illness she was tirelessly active in
union work. Those of us who know the facts would claim
that Brenda's war effort was surpassed by very few women
who served in Civil Defence, and it is at least surprising
that her work was not officially and suitably recognized. She
herself would certainly be the last person to look back upon
the past; yet she could do so with genuine pride, knowing

that through her efforts so much has been done to make easier the lot of suffering men and women.

☆   ☆   ☆

NANCY BUDGETT is a very independent spirit who has that one essential quality of leadership which makes her capable not merely of leading herself but of following another's lead with courage and determination. An invaluable person to have in Casualties Union is Nancy because she is one of those people who have the happy ability of looking at others with a perceptive but unjaundiced eye. Those who know her well are proud to have her friendship, and all her many associates learn to expect in their dealings with her that spirit of understanding helpfulness which gives without stint and takes little in return.

It was these qualities that led her originally into the suffragette movement and which later transformed her into a probation officer. She certainly believes ardently in the equality of the sexes, and proceeds to justify her claims by her own devoted service and efficiency.

Nancy Budgett has a difficult job to do for the union, in apportioning the requests for assistance received from other organizations and making sure that these are met by the best skill available. Her tact has so far always overcome those minor jealousies which think, 'I ought to have been given that job in place of him.' Yes, the union is well served in this sphere, but Nancy (who is a founder member) is not merely an administrator — far from it. Her planning and staging of accidents is always apt and appropriate; her own acting as a 'casualty', while she would rate it as the least of her accomplishments, can often catch one right out, as one dashes to render assistance quite unnecessarily; and her make-up technique is very good — in fact as good as any that the writer has ever seen.

☆   ☆   ☆

ROY STOKES, B.E.M., is a special person. There has never been time to ask how tall he is, but he always strikes me as being huge. He has a tremendous grin and a large and generous mind. His voice is quiet, but it is well worth while to listen to anything he has to say, for he is the right type to serve on a committee. What is more, he has a valuable sense of humour.

His casualty work is excellent. He never over-acts and willingly takes orders from his producer. On the research side, his knowledge of mechanics has enabled him to make some useful gadgets that simplify the staging of 'accidents'. He himself is a good organizer, and produces First Aid problems for our annual competitions. this involves him in a tremendous amount of paper-work, producing marking sheets and so on, and also entails the handling of a large staff of helpers in addition to the 'casualties'.

I have never seen him ruffled; and to know one is going to work with or for Roy gives one the comforting feeling that everything will certainly be all right.

☆   ☆   ☆

PERCY SARGEANT. All the qualities of the perfect Secretary seem to be present in Percy Sargeant, who despite very considerable commitments in Civil Defence and a responsible full-time job, manages to turn up to every committee meeting, including most of the sub-committees too, and to produce facts and figures without hesitation.

A founder member of the union, he is an extremely capable Instructor and Producer in addition, and is responsible for a great deal of the interest that Civil Defence is now showing in the work of the union.

He is not only always there, but is unfailingly patient and understanding, and — most happily for the committee members — always the same. It is so seldom nowadays that one can rely upon one's friends and associates in this way. So often one has to think that pressure of work, health and many other reasons are the cause of a certain lack of cordiality in greeting, etc., but in Percy Sargeant there is always the same quiet, courteous greeting, and attention to queries, which one comes to associate with him.

In appearance he is tall, thinnish, with hair showing he has numerous worries to account for its whitening colour, and the abstracted look of the scholar about him — he

147

Percy G. Sargeant
Hon. General Secretary

could easily be taken for a schoolmaster with his kindly eyes and charming smile. His dress reflects the same attention to detail, always correct. With all this, there is quite a twinkle of fun in his eyes, and a capacity to extract the most out from a situation.

Long may he continue to exercise his tact and efficiency as the union's secretary.

☆　　☆　　☆

HARRY DAVIES. Our earliest recollection of Councillor Harry Davies is of a wiry little man with a bright complexion and a mop of thick, black, curly hair, and a deep sense of justice. When he thought criticism was unwarranted, his face went purple, sparks flashed from his dark eyes and the curls rose, balancing precariously his tin hat, while he let forth a tirade of Welsh-English at incredible speed.

A born leader, Harry Davies has dedicated his life to the service of his fellow men. Responsive, affectionate, keen and loyal, he led a part-time Civil Defence rescue party during the war, He trained them well and led them fearlessly. Difficulties and dangers were not new to him. In his earlier

Harry Davis in the Chair,
is supported by Eric Claxton and Percy Sargeant

life as a Welsh miner he had known the misery of tightening his belt and of standing in the soup queues. After he left the coalfields he found his spare time recreation by becoming a first class county football referee.

Harry worked hard in the first general elections after the war addressing meetings at street corners in support of his candidate. No one could doubt his sincerity, and now he is serving his second term of office as Councillor for Egham. A founder member of Casualties Union he has continued to work with us in addition to all his other activities.

Fighting all the way, with study and reading and practice, he has made himself a good public speaker and an accomplished chairman. As chairman of the general management and executive committees of the union Harry Davies is making an outstanding contribution to the development of the union.

ERIC CLAXTON. Whether one believes in astrological influence or not, there is no getting away from the fact that all the qualities and gifts associated with the sign Aquarius have been showered upon Eric Claxton. If one is a doubter it is surely extraordinary coincidental that he was born

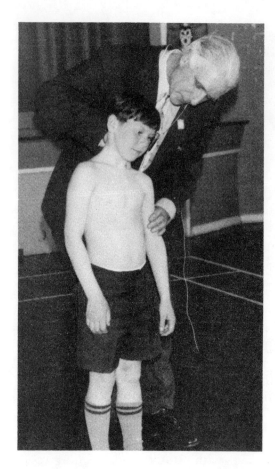

Helping Bobby White to adopt the shoulder shape for a fractured clavicle

between January 21st and February 20th. Idealist, reformer, and leader, he IS the union personified. If, at times, he soars completely over our heads, and is perhaps a shade impractical, he nevertheless sets the course, and nothing short of the best is good enough.

With all this idealism, his personality is so friendly, cheerful and helpful that one's doubts vanish, dissolved by that 'I know that you can do it' attitude. Surely that is the test of true leadership — faith in one's team, which in turn produces faith in one's purpose, and eventually in oneself.

It is unusual to find a visionary possessed of technical ability which formed the foundation on which to build the

Cyril Wallis becomes a
casualty at Barnet Hill
House

vision that was to become Casualties Union. It would have
been no use using faked casualties in the Rescue School at
Leatherhead without the knowledge required to stage the
rescue work with safety both for first aiders and for
casualties — hence the insistence on the necessity for both
doctor and civil engineer on the committee of the
organization.

The fact that the union today is still increasing its
membership, when most voluntary organizations are finding
it difficult to keep their numbers up, is largely due to the
unstinting and unflagging energies of its founder member
and chairman of council. It is extremely difficult to fall by
the way while he almost kills himself with work for the
cause. The only fault one can find with him is that he just
doesn't know when he's beaten: and, after all, that is the
best way to success.

☆　　☆　　☆

A. CYRIL WALLIS. Although he is a founder member and has been with us all along, nobody knows what the A. stands for; he's just Cyril to us all. One would like to think that Cyril is typical of Casualties Union, but it is quite certain that Casualties Union is typical of Cyril.

He lives in a wonderful old house in Surrey and is a lover of village life. We all thought that he had 'retired' in the usual sense of the word, but now find that in addition to being the stage-manager 'noises off' for the local dramatic and sporting events, he is holding a very responsible job supervising and demonstrating an experimental engine. We now know that Cyril, though of a retiring nature, will never retire!

Nothing is too much trouble for him, and no details will be overlooked. He will question you for hours just to make certain he has got the intention quite clear. He will make certain also, by direct personal contact, even if it means cycling for miles, that everyone else knows too.

Cyril became a senior instructor. With those qualities how could he escape? For his special work he discovered bread plastic and specializes in 'blood' colourings and consistencies, blood pumps, and mechanical devices. He is the Wal half of the Walcon method of transforming a 'closed' into an 'open' fracture. Cyril is a craftsman — a lover of things done well. At Barnett Hill you will always find him down the copse chopping his thigh with a bill-hook.

There are some others whom I would have liked to see included in this list, but sadly their deaths intervened before an opportunity arose. I presume therefore to include their obituaries in this chapter.

ROBIN GREY. It is with profound regret that we record the death of Hilda Gwendolen Gray, on 23rd April, 1953 in Tasmania. Mrs. Gray will be remembered by founder members as Robin Young, the war widow of a naval doctor killed in the Battle of Britain.

Robin had an infectious enthusiasm and during the war years she was undoubtedly one of the union's best ambassadors. She had a soft voice and a ready smile and great charm. Robin cast a peacefulness around her and her bubbling laugh and her faith in the ultimate victory of good brought comfort to many.

One bitter day towards the end of the war, Robin volunteered to be buried for hours in a small cavity in the piles of debris at the Rescue School at Leatherhead. We used to tease Robin about an ancient fur coat known as 'Tattie'. Casually she asked whether it would be proper to wear it on this bitter occasion. She was the 'missing casualty' and was bound to be the last to be rescued. This was readily agreed — but none of us knew that Robin suffered greatly from a poor circulation and had to sleep under an electric blanket.

After the war Robin married the Rev. Alan Gray and emigrated to Tasmania, where together they ran Christ's Hospital at Hobart. In recognition of her services to Casualties Union Robin was appointed an honorary member in 1950. She was a grand person.

☆　　☆　　☆

C.J.M. ADIE. Time has borne away another founder member who was a friend, colleague and councillor to many wartime members who knew little about him except the kindly measured words with which he replied to all remarks.

Many of us first met Mr. Adie as chief warden for Egham Civil Defence. At the end of the war he undertook the duties of hon. treasurer of the union, which he carried out meticulously until ill health made him resign from active membership in 1949.

He was a great oarsman and rowed for Cambridge in 1900 when his boat won by twenty lengths, equalling the record for the race. He was a schoolmaster — more than that — he was a housemaster at Eton College. When the Provost of Eton invited us to hold our first post-war reunion on Fellows' Eyot one recognized the warm regard in which Mr. Adie was held although he had been retired for a number of years.

37

Annual Conference at Bedford College 1954

Nancy Budgett gets us off to a good start with a bit of sales talk.

PLASTIC PARODY
With apologies to Lewis Carroll

'You are cold, C.U. member,' the first aider said,
    'And your face is exceedingly white,
With faint shades of blue, and sweat on your brow,
    You're in an uncomfortable plight!'

'In my youth,' said the member, 'I made up my face
    And practised the art of deception,
To help the C.D. and first aiders besides,
    And this one is not an exception.'

'You are queer!' said the helper, with Plasticine, paint,
    Portex and powders and porridge,
You make all the difference from fitness to faint!
    How d'you get this peculiar knowledge?'

'On grease paint and acting I found many tips,
    And how to make burns with face tissue,
Contained in the Journal, four copies a year,
    Allow me to sell you an issue!'

'We learn,' said the patient, 'each aspect to show
    In this acting and staging affair,

And this is the reason we do all this stuff
So that you'll treat your injured with care.'

N.P.M.B.

The third annual conference was a friendly and constructive affair. It was well attended, and afforded opportunities for discussion and exchange of views between headquarters and groups of members, which only the wide representation on this occasion could provide. It was our great pleasure that the president, Dr. Glyn Hughes was able to preside at all the sessions.

The theme of the conference was 'The Standard to be set for Casualty Portrayal,' and a series of speakers worked out a pattern of progress from initiation to examination, indicating the trials, responsibilities and aims of each grade of membership.

Mrs. G. R. Payne (Member — Norwich) described her experience as *probationer;* how interest had been aroused in Norwich by a headquarters demonstration and a Study Circle had been formed. They shared the difficulties common to most Study Circles — ignorance of the appearance of injuries, and enlisting the interest of sympathetic doctors, who did not perhaps at first realize that they were setting out to study the behaviour of injured people. Mrs. Payne was in no doubt that the essential aids for probationers to reach proficiency were a leader with courage and determination, medical advice and visits from senior members of the union for encouragement.

Mrs. D. E. Hancox (Instructor — Staffordshire) put into words what most of us could echo in our experience, that after one had qualified as a *member,* and the first flush of triumph at having passed the proficiency test had faded, one's sense of perspective returned and brought with it a more critical interpretation of our aims and standards. What had seemed good enough to a beginner no longer compared favourably with one's growing experience of what injuries looked like and how injured people behaved. Constant practice in the elements of acting and false tissue application were essential, and for this purpose weekly meetings were ideal, with private 'off-time' acting practice in addition.

Harry Davies (Senior Instructor — Headquarters) paid tribute to the Study Circle notes and method of training, for by this means and with the indispensable help of local doctors, many members had reached *instructor* grade with very little other guide from H.Q. The instructor was the guardian of standard for the branch, and the local ambassador for Casualties Union in all dealings with kindred societies. Sometimes through a tangle of misunderstanding of C.U. principles the instructor had to compromise with user organisations whose standards of realism were not all-embracing. The request for the cycle accident in the drawing-room, or the scald from the empty kettle, call for tactful handling to obtain a result satisfactory to all parties. The final judge of standard was often the first-aider, and it was for his training in handling more confidently the casualty of the future that the instructor held the responsibility.

Eric Claxton (Founder of the Union and Chairman of the Council) gave a clear outline of the policy that guided the appointment of the *senior instructor*. By way of nomination, interview and the commissioning of some research which would further the use of C.U. technique, the committee sought to place the highest responsibilities in the hands of experienced instructors who had the qualities of leadership. Basically they were persons competent to train instructors, but it was hoped that they would prove themselves to be more than that. They should have sound technical ability, though as the elders of the movement, they were expected to take responsibility for the development of the union rather than as practitioners of the art themselves. They must be people of vision who understood the policy of the union and were convinced of the importance of its work. Ideally they should be persona grata with everybody so that relations with kindred societies could become increasingly friendly as time passed. Noted for imagination, courage and understanding, the guiding hands to the discouraged and the over-confident. And being entirely selfless, gain only by giving, and in so doing, only give more.

We all felt that we fell far short of Mr. Claxton's ideal, but we were grateful to him for holding this standard before us. He went on to refer to the standard he would expect to be demanded by senior instructors. In the light of all the qualities, there was *but one standard* — that the behaviour of trained 'casualties', their appearance and environment, must convince that an accident has happened and that someone is hurt. It is an *absolute standard without exception.* Nevertheless, by those same qualities the senior instructor would know that new members who were keen would gain experience and proficiency as they went on, provided the absolute standard was held before them in a sympathetic, tactful and constructive manner.

Dr. J. C. Turnbull (Altrincham Medical Adviser) brought a wealth of humour and sound advice to his statement of the *Medical Adviser's* point of view. He reiterated the importance of every circle having a helpful medical adviser, preferably one whose professional dignity would allow him to be an *acting* as well as an active member. A doctor whose experience was surgical and whose working hours were regular (e.g. a factory M.O.) would be most likely to be interested and attend the circle meetings often. His criticism should be ruthless (remembering that C.U. Standard is 100%) and members should accept it in the spirit in which it was given. Praise, issued with reserve and evenly bestowed, should be related to the member's own ability and not compared with others. It was advisable to return frequently to the training notes and to check with the M.O. that 'star turns' were as good now as when they first performed. It seemed fair that the circle should use their M.O. as a key to hospitals, books, films, clinics, for medical, dental and other technical information.

Dr. Turnbull found that a sense of humour, boundless enthusiasm, the patient of Job, an expanding car, a poker face and a forgiving wife were all necessary adjuncts to his medical qualifications in his capacity as medical adviser to a Study Circle. We enjoyed his enthusiastic approach to his subject enormously, especially when he said that his work for C.U. had made him look more observantly at his own patients!

There were about seventy members present at the practical session on cases for the teaching of nursing, produced by senior instructor Pat Loarridge. There was a patient with extensive burns of her back being received into hospital and put to bed; a drainage tube had been removed from a lung abess and the wound had to be dressed and bandaged; first stages of measles; tracheotomy tube in position, to teach cleaning and general care; and a blind patient, partially paralysed, to teach approach and special nursing technique.

At the Saturday morning session Mr. Claxton spoke on the draft proposals for the re-organization of the constitution of the union. Most of us were very much impressed with the clarity of thought behind the proposals, and the width of vision which made allowances for many far-reaching changes to accommodate the developing use of our technique and the increasing demand for our awards. It was the desire of the conference that every member should have the opportunity of studying the draft before further action was considered.

The closing session of the conference took the form of an open forum at which a team of senior instructors dealt with questions on many subjects. Matters of organization and policy jostled with problems of publicity to make a very interesting session for the audience and a very gruelling hour for the team. Some of the hares that were raised are still being chased, and some of the questions and answers will echo through the pages of the Journal for many years to come.

38

Competitions — The Worm's Eye View

Trophies are won and lost over our heads and conveyed each year in triumph to fresh lodgings, to be photographed, stroked and polished by proud hands for another twelve months. In the course of many battles we stand in for the victims of accidents who have their necks twisted and their aching limbs squeezed and dropped by men and women whose wits desert them to give place to 'competition nerves'. Backstage we say to one another, 'Surely they wouldn't do that at a real accident, and yet we look and behave like real casualties.' And so we take you each year to a natural setting where we hope that the crowd of spectators will not seem much like an audience that they prevent you from behaving like real first-aiders and treating the 'accident' as though it had just happened.

The Pool of London, King's Cross Station, Holford Square Flats, Hendon Airfield and now Pinewood Film Studios. The site is chosen first and the situation designed to fit, but the two are closely related to simulate atmosphere and cultivate awareness of natural resources and hazards. What of the weather? You will agree that it plays the same part as it does in real accidents, just another feature against which the practised first-aider protects the patient to ward off shock. What of the audience? Most accidents in public places attract a crowd, which, if it is not controlled becomes a natural hazard!

In a Casualties Union competition the judges are asked to

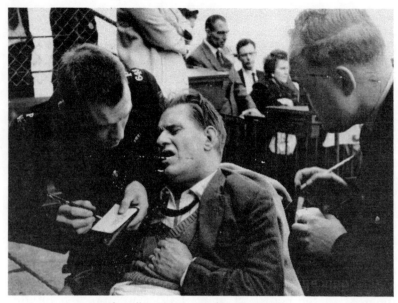
A police team examines a casualty

command a limited field of observation, so their task is
specialized and concentrated. You must not tell them what
you are doing, because they can see and they miss nothing.
In the first aid contest the two doctors decide on all matters
medical and concerned with the improvement or worsening
of the patient's condition. A lay judge, well versed in the
finer differences between the methods of the teaching
societies watches all the technical points of dressing,
bandaging and splinting which can be decided purely on
text-book knowledge. A transport officer decides on the
stretcher work and loading efficiency. As none of these
people are supposed to be there in an official capacity, the
teams must find out all they can from the staging, history,
signs and symptoms of the casualty by questioning, looking
and feeling. This is very important because the casualty
does some of the judging too, by awarding marks for the
feeling of the treatment. There is so much of which only the
casualty can be aware — the degree of confidence in the
touch of the first-aiders, the support or discomfort of the
bandages and lifting. A real ambulance is available, so there

is minimum of make-believe about it.

In the diagnosis section two members of each team examine a series of casualties in exactly the way they ought to examine a really injured or ill person, but without treatment. They must look and question, and feel and listen. They may help the casualty to move or may ask him if he can move himself, but whatever is done must only take one minute. Then there is one minute and a half for reflection and writing a list of history, signs and symptoms such as could be given in describing the situation to a doctor over the 'phone. Marks are increased for giving a specific diagnosis in addition, but by sub-dividing the answers in this way it is made impossible to get more than half the available marks by just guessing, without making a thorough examination. The emphasis is laid on the first-aiders' ability to size up a situation from the setting of the accident, the posture and remarks of the patient, or the surrounding clues. The answer papers are corrected under the guidance of doctors and the marks gained by the pair of competitors are added to the marks of their colleagues on the first aid set to make a team total.

There is nothing elaborate about the settings or the accidents. The only advantages Casualties Union claims for its methods are economy in production, a stimulating atmosphere of realism, and while providing a common meeting ground for all those interested in the advancement of first aid, giving an opportunity of seeing and using the living training equipment.

Our hopes for Pinewood were threefold. That you would all regard it as an important event in your training programme and not just another competition. That you would tell your friends to come and watch; that you would tell us your ideas for improving the competition, and enter again next year. Our guest of honour on this occasion was Sir Parker Morris, Ll.B., town clerk and Civil Defence controller designate to the City of Westminster.

This was indeed a most important year for Casualties Union because for the first time we staged regional eliminating rounds for the Buxton Trophy competition. Ninety-six teams entered and contests were held in Truro; Winchester; Wallington, Surrey; St. Albans; Stroud; Birm-

A parachutist casualty

Photo by courtesy of Newcastle Evening Chronicle

ingham; Norwich; Altrincham; Darlington and Newcastle. There was one entry from Scotland which gained a bye into the final contest. This was a tremendous undertaking for so young an organization.

The winners of the Buxton Trophy were S.J.A.B., Hull Docks; the First Aid Trophy was won by N.C.B. Desford Colliery and the Diagnosis Trophy was won by I.C.I. Alkali Division, Northwich. Undoubtedly a most encouraging result.

☆ ☆ ☆

In subsequent years it was routine for contests in the regions to select representative teams. In 1955, there were a hundred and twenty-five teams taking part including two teams from Scotland and one from Ireland. A new trophy presented to the union by the Institute of Civil Defence was open for competition and was to be held for one year by the team predominantly of the opposite sex to the winners gaining highest aggregate points.

For the finals we were guests of Sir John Stephenson and members of the Eastern Gas Board at their Ponders End Gas Works. There were twenty-four teams competing in the final. Our guests of honour were the Rt. Hon. Iain MacLeod and Mrs. MacLeod and the team winning the Buxton Trophy also won the First Aid Trophy. They were Stafford County Police; B.R.C.S. Dumbarton won the I.C.D. Trophy, while N.C.B. Desford Colliery won the Diagnosis Trophy.

☆ ☆ ☆

We were privileged for the first time to have a sponsor for the programme in 1956 when Messrs. Arthur Guinness, Son & Co., (Park Royal) Ltd. generously gave us programmes for both eliminating and final rounds and we were most happy to ornament these programmes with some of their advertising motifs — the zoo keeper astonished at seeing a kangeroo with his bottle of Guinness in his pouch — and the seal doing tricks with a football. There were a hundred and seventeen teams entering and fifteen regional eliminating contests leading to the selection of twenty-four teams in the finals. These were held at the Army Mobile Defence Corps Depot, at Epsom, Surrey.

Epsom attracted the largest crowd we had ever had at our competition finals. We had real Casualties Union weather, cold and dry, with the smell of the neighbouring sewage farm to savour the wind! But strangely enough both members and visitors were all so busy and engrossed with what they had to do and see that hardly anyone noticed it and after all we had been at the gas works the previous year!

There was much to see that year. A new range of competitions had been staged for spectators themselves to 'have a go', an opportunity that a good many visitors appeared to welcome. There was blindfold bandaging, stretcher carrying, and diagnosis. Perhaps these could be developed in future years. There was also a series of demonstrations by various societies and services, including our hosts The Mobile Defence Corps, who were rescuing casualties from heights in bombed buildings. The National Hospital Service Reserve were receiving and treating special casualties, and two or three of our members were staging domestic accidents in co-operation with the Royal Society for the Prevention of Accidents in a special side-show to encourage propaganda in safety first in the home.

We were charmed to welcome as our guests of honour, Miss Pat Hornsby-Smith, M.P., Parliamentary Secretary to the Ministry of Health, and Miss Durning Lawrence, who was a Trustee of the Aston Trust, our benefactors. The interest that they both took in the union's activities made it a great pleasure to show them the work we do and present to them the people who do the work.

We were also happy to have the company of high-ranking United States military medical officers, who expressed their approbation of the skilled patient. The party included general S. B. Hayes, Director General of United States Army Medical Forces, and G. L. Gorby who holds the same position in the U.S. Army Medical Forces in Germany.

The Ministry of Food Flying Squad and the W.V.S. catered for us most admirably.

Mrs V.I. van der Does, Hon. General Secretary, International Federation of Pedestrians is Guest of Honour at Sandown Park

39

Uncle Sam Sees for Himself

When Uncle Sam hears about something he wants, he goes all out to get it. Within days of the event at Epsom, the American Embassy 'phoned asking urgently for a brief history of the union. We had nothing with which to accommodate their request so I compiled 'The Brief History' and this was voted to be entirely satisfactory. It would, however, get out of date through the years that followed.

That was why Colonel Vincent I. Hack of the United States Army Medical Services School, Houston, Texas, and Colonel Jack Walden of the Surgeon-General's staff in Washington, D.C., were flown over specially to watch London branch giving a demonstration of Casualties Union technique on 20th February, 1957.

This was a unique occasion for us upon two counts. England had yet another result of much research to show America, and the B.B.C. sent a reporter along. The fact that the reporter passed out cold after seeing the third injury in no way detracted from the value of the demonstration. It was a comfort that he recovered sufficiently (by dint of much cossetting and a double brandy) to obtain a tape-recording of Colonel Hack's appreciation of C.U. technique for broadcast to North America the following day.

It was a great joy to all of us who took part that our president, Dr. Glyn Hughes, was with us throughout the whole evening. In just over an hour sixteen casualties, ranging from a minor cut, to haemorrhages, fractures, insensibility, hysteria and epilepsy had been demonstrated. Oh! and there was also a gentleman gradually falling asleep in a corner of the room through sheer boredom! — or was he planted? There was also a staged incident dealt with by a team of Red Cross women and a demonstration of a Study Circle in action.

I sold the goods with a running commentary and it was no time before our two Colonels were handling the cases for themselves. Colonel Walden wanted to try out a lot more conditions than had been prepared and tried briefing a probationer for pleurisy, with results which satisfied him. Their attention never faltered, they were entranced with all that they saw and were with us all the way.

David Holmes recorded an interview with Colonel Hack after the performance. In reply to an enquiry as to his reactions, our American guests said he thought it all quite terrific. He went on to say, 'In the United States we definitely do not have the whole type of training that you have in your simulated casualty. Primarily we are impressed by the acting that goes with your technique, and we think it would do a great deal in augmenting the training programmes in our Army. We only have a fake type of skin which is not nearly so realistic as what you produce here with your materials. We were sent here to get this and we shall definitely be using it with military mass casualties. In fact I can visualize that civilianwise in the United States it will prove very dramatic and effective, and that would be most important. We have heard of it, but this is the first time we have seen it in operation.'

We offered our help at every stage of its development in both army and civilian fields.

40

Challenge From Within a Sewer Manhole

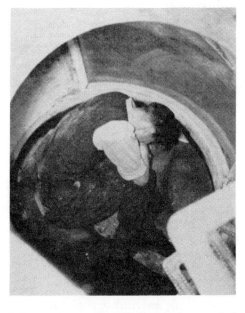

An unconscious man at
the bottom of a standard
sewer manhole

The union was fully conscious of the need for Civil Rescue
in peace time as well as in war and believed that there were
a number of problems which required more study as well as
practice. In an endeavour to stimulate interest in such
problems the union proposed to hold a study/contest on
Casualties Union Day, Sunday, 6th October, 1957, at
London University Sports Ground, Motspur Park, when the
final round of the Buxton Trophy would be held.

The judges view the situation through the perspex window

Industrial concerns and other bodies were asked to study the problem of rescue of an unconscious man (concussion) from an eight foot deep sewer manhole of standard pattern. It was proposed to construct a concrete manhole with a transparent window so that judges, doctors and engineers, could observe the methods used. The patient, a trained casualty, would be able to make observations afterwards but behave throughout the rescue as if he were completely unconscious by concussion.

The rules were simple. It was open to teams from any firm or organization, without limit to number of members but it was expected that only one person could get into the manhole at one time with the patient. No time limit was set but because of the condition of the patient no team was expected to exceed fifteen minutes. Teams were to provide their own equipment but a stretcher and blankets would be provided — test to end when the patient was blanketed and laid on stretcher. Each team provided a written statement of their method for the judges to study one week in advance and the team must adhere to the method described. The contest was judged upon a system of points allocated for control, speed, simplicity, efficiency and gentleness of the operation.

There was an entry fee of ten shillings and the winners were to hold the Jarvis Rose Bowl for one year. The notice given allowed teams a period of six months to practice and seek out their best method.

There were twenty teams competing in this first year and the most successful teams were Brislington Ambulance, S.J.A.B., John Dickinson Fire Brigade and Romford Civil Defence 'B'.

The study/contests were continued for two more years and competitors had the advantage of studying the report(s) for the previous contest(s). The manhole cover and frame were changed each year to ensure that this had no over-riding effect upon the problem.

The contest was widely advertised so that employees of local authorities and industrial concerns might study and practise for several months prior to each contest.

The contests were held on Casualties Union Day at the following venues: 1957 — London University Sports Ground, Motspur Park, Surrey. The weather was fine and the benching was kept dry. No special direction was given as to the number of men to be included in a team but points were awarded for the smallness of the team. No time limit was set. No special direction was given as to clothing to be worn by competitors or casualty; 1958 — George Cohen 600 Group Depot, Wood Lane, London W12. The weather turned wet. The benching had been made greasy at the start and the patient's clothing became sodden and impregnated with grease. The patient was clothed in overall, boots and equipped as a sewer workman. The leader was required to wear a safety belt and lifeline. Time limit ten minutes; 1959 — Orpington Hospital, Orpington, Kent. The weather was fine and the benching was greasy. The casualty was a different person from the previous two years.

The manhole was constructed above ground and the chamber was illuminated by a perspex window, through which the judges were able to study the operations. This

The complete manhole set-up overground.
This was used in 1957-58-59

also provided light for the rescue-worker in the chamber. It also enabled teams to observe the methods demonstrated by other teams, which was an essential part of the study. To prevent any team having an unfair advantage in a particular year's contest, each team was required to deposit a written description of the method they intended to adopt. They were penalized by the loss of points if the method demonstrated did not conform.

The judges comprised engineers, doctors, and, of course, the 'casualty', several of them served for more than one year. They came from many areas where they held responsible posts.

It is well to look at the entries and the results which are eloquent in themselves.

	1957	1958	1959
Number of teams	20	22	23
Winners	Brislington Amb. S.J.A.B.	John Dickinson Fire Brigade	H.M. Dockyard Chatham
Second	John Dickinson Fire Brigade	B.O.A.C. Fire Post 'A'	Staffordshire County C.D.
Third	Romford C.D. 'B'	H.M. Dockyard Chatham	B.O.A.C. Fire Post 'A'
Winner's time	7 minutes	5 min. 30 sec.	3 min. 50 sec.
Fastest time	6 min. 30 sec.	4 min. 15 sec.	2 min. 17 sec.

The timing gives one indication of the progress achieved during the series of study/contests. This is more significant when it is appreciated that the contest was made progressively more difficult. One comes to the conclusion that it was well worth while undertaking.

The judges reported that the criterion for a standard method should be safety, simplicity and speed. Equipment must be easily applied to an unconscious man of any weight without risk of aggravating injuries. They observed that the problem would normally occur when a sewer gang of two men has an accident causing one of them to become unconscious at the bottom of a manhole. A larger gang would have more resources, but it was to the more severe situation that attention was given.

The second sewer man recruits two passers-by to haul out the victim, while he enters into the manhole to secure the harness onto the casualty below and then directs and controls the whole operation from below. In the course of the three contests many different types of equipment were used; most of them aimed at lifting the man out head first; a smaller number sought to raise him feet first. The best head first introduced a cane-reinforced bodice with support for the head using a face mask with remote breathing tube. The most efficient feet first needed a figure of eight strap to encircle ankles and insteps with a belt for the waist and an adjustable link between the two, so that in lifting the weight is shared by the waist as well as the ankles.

Finally the judges recommended both methods, with a bias in favour of the feet first method, where there is no serious injury to head or legs on the grounds of speed, simplicity, and safety (including the self-clearance of vomit). The cane-reinforced bodice is preferred for use when serious injury has occurred to head or legs.

The committee summed up the project: Two simple, safe and effective methods have emerged from these contests. The feet first method, which is quicker, simpler and copes more effectively with the medical requirements, is clearly the method to choose in all cases where the unconscious man has not been *severely* injured on head or legs. In those cases, the head first method, which takes longer, is satisfactory when sound equipment is available. Between them these two methods appear to be capable of dealing with all likely situations.

The committee therefore considers that the purpose of these study/contests has been achieved and they do not propose to stage further tests. They have prepared this document as their final report, which they commend to all authorities and persons responsible for men working in sewers. The committee recommends that each sewer gang be issued with the equipment described in this report and be trained in its use. Although this contest is to be discontinued, it is hoped that its simple but practical character will stimulate local authorities to stage district or regional contests to develop skill in using these two methods, so that they may be ready at a moment's notice to act in emergency.

Allow me a postscript to this item. This problem could not have been created without a limp unconscious person and showed therefore the help that a trained patient may give to studies of that kind. Ron Williams, the casualty, was stiff and sore after his ordeal, but his report was a triumph of balanced judgement showing the strength and weakness of each method used to rescue him. He did it for over forty teams in the first two years of the contest and would have done it for the third year but for the fact that we desired to introduce a taller and heavier man. A. Sayer, his successor in agony, was equally courageous and I was very proud of them both. A splendid investigation which was worth every bit of the effort put into it.

41

On The Floor With Our Gallant Doctors

Dr John S. Binning. Medical
adviser Liverpool Street Branch

Dr. Binning was a man of many parts. He was one of
British Rail's medical officers, he was a high ranking officer
in the T.A. Medical Wing, he was medical adviser to the
Liverpool Street (British Railways) Branch of Casualties
Union.

One bright morning in March, 1957, related Dr. Binning, I was watching the passengers embarking on the Danish mailboat at Parkeston Quay. A voice said, 'Are you bringing Casualties Union down here for the competition this year?'

I turned to find one of the longshoremen, a member of the local first aid class. I said I would be delighted to do so but so far I had not been asked.

'Well, we would like to see them again. They were a great help.' He paused for a moment. 'They are all professional actors and actresses, aren't they?' I replied that they were not, but that they would be pleased to know their standard of performance had suggested such a status. I thanked my friend for his kind words and in due course had great pleasure in telling the members concerned.

A few weeks later I went down to Parkeston Quay for the annual local competition, not to judge it but to play the part of the patient. This was kept secret until the actual starting hour, and not a few team members were startled to see their one time examiner, mentor and coach on the floor. However, all went well, but my impressions of that afternoon confirm what I have observed as a judge of first aid practice over a number of years. The rough handling of a patient, particularly by male teams, a thing which is always being criticised by competition judges, still goes on.

Rough handling will frighten the patient and aggravate the degree of shock, adding insult to injury. It is clear that the trained casualty must yell his head off and go on yelling until he is treated more humanely. Otherwise our teaching is not having its full effect. There is no excuse for letting it continue; after all, not so long ago, the treatment of shock was shamefully performed, but, by criticism, both kindly and sharp, by example and by practice, we have seen improvement. In the same way rough handling could be eliminated.

The women's teams always do handle their patient more gently, just as they are better at reassurance, speaking to the patient at the time. Nothing annoys a casualty, who has been knocked down and dragged under a 'bus, so much as to be told, 'You're all right,' when in fact he is probably half dead.

Words of reassurance should be continuously spoken and quietly spoken and on that April afternoon on the floor at Parkeston, I felt that the men had a lot to learn from the women in this matter. Another thing I noted was how alarming it is for the patient to be examined by the fingers rather than the whole hand. Palpation should be with the whole hand, smoothly and gently passed down a limb or across the abdomen. Five finger exercises can be both painful and alarming.

The lifting of an injured person needs careful team work. If it is not done well the patient becomes alarmed and thinks he is going to fall. It may not be appreciated by all first aiders that when one is lying on the floor persons standing around appear foreshortened, rather like giants, whose erratic or clumsy movement will further increase the fear and terror of the patient.

After this very friendly first aid competition was over a team member said, 'Ah, now you know what it is like to be a patient.' But in fact, I already knew, having learned the hard way when I broke my humerus while training in 1942. I was gently handled on the whole, but my terror at being lifted on a stretcher by two undersized medical orderlies is remembered vividly to this day.

In respect of these matters which I have mentioned, I think it is necessary for trained members of Casualties Union to react violently to rough handling, to the infliction of needless discomfort by thoughtless action on the part of the first aider.

We are out to help that great body of voluntary workers, and I am sure that they do not do the wrong things purposely, but simply through excitement, ignorance or forgetfulness. They will learn in due course: our purpose in Casualties Union is to help to teach the first aiders by realistic reaction to handling and treatment. It is better that they should learn on 'guinea pigs' rather than the real casualties.

Back in the Army with Dr. John Turnbull, *reported by our frustrated, female, field photographer.*

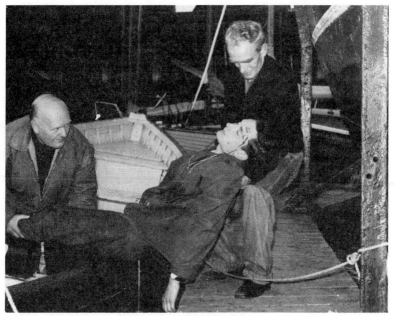

Hit by the swinging boom

We had been asked to supply two male casualties for each day of an R.A.M.C. (T.A.) Ambulance Shield competition. On the Saturday, part of the competition was held in the drill hall, with two members of each of the competing teams, five teams in all, to attend each incident, one casualty only. On the Sunday, the other members of the teams were to take part in a stretcher-bearing exercise, with one casualty, under fire, and over difficult terrain. As our newly fledged male members (apart from our medical adviser) had never been out on their own before, it was arranged that I should accompany them, as instructor and maker-up, photographer, prisoner's friend and call boy. It was all to be run on strictly military lines, and the C.O. had asked that I should appear in uniform (B.R.C.S., Branch Officer), so that I should not get thrown out as a female civilian by some over-enthusiastic sentry.

SATURDAY. Frank and Alex were taking part, and we were all looking forward to an afternoon's fun. We were received with deference by the R.S.M., and given the M.I.

Room to use as a dressing room. When we had parked all our kit, the chaps were escorted by another W.O. to the clothing stores, and there they were 'fitted' out with a complete set of denims, shirts, socks and boots.

Frank had served in the Army, and Alex in the R.A.F., so neither were put out by the lack of cut in these garments. Frank's incident was that he was supposed to have been 'fixing' a fuse, with an unsuitable screwdriver, while standing on a step-ladder. He was to sustain a severe electric-shock, fall off the ladder, and break his left wrist. When found by the team, he was lying on his face, near the ladder, also fallen, with the screwdriver and the fuse nearby. The door of the fusebox was left open.

His facial make-up looked particularly convincing in the very light drillhall (practically the whole roof was glass). The Colles fracture none of us was completely happy about. At rehearsals, bread putty did not seem to be of the standard of Miss Nancy Budgett, and it had been decided to revert to plasticine, well-collodioned, to withstand handling . . . did I say handling? As it is not regarded seemly to criticize in public, I will make no comment on the first aid.

Frank had one extremely difficult moment in remaining 'out', when a voice which he knew very well, and which he hadn't heard for twelve years, addressed him by name — an old friend from Frank's old mob in Wartime Palestine. To his everlasting credit, he gave no sign of recognition 'til the incident was well over.

Alex had a different incident. He was to have been 'on maintenance' beneath a three tonner, lying on his back, with a large spanner, attending to the nuts of the differential. One foot lay under the near-rear wheel. Some 'adjectival clot' (I misquote Alex) was to get into the driver's cabin, switch on, and start the engine and release the handbrake. The wheel was to roll back onto Alex's foot. Alex's yells were to be sufficient for the driver to proceed no further — though he was not to switch off the engine. Alex's injuries were to be fractures of two or three metatarsals, and abrasions caused by the deep tread of the tyre pressing on the laced-up portion of the boot. The fractures were suggested by extensive bruising, and the abrasions formed a suitable pattern.

Comments which were made in public, were to the effect that the teams were somewhat disconcerted at having apparently real casualties to deal with, behaving like injured people, and not the usual luggage label variety used heretofore. The comments were unprintable.

SUNDAY. The stretcher bearing exercise was arranged in a bit of natural parkland, five miles north of Manchester. By name, 'Boggart Hole Clough', and for those of you who do not know what that means — when freely translated it becomes 'Fairies' Dell'. A Boggart is a Lancashire fairy. 'Clough' in Lancashire, is a steep, smallish valley, between two hills. What the troops called it that Sunday, had nothing to do with fairies . . .

On Saturday night previously, there had fallen the first rain, believe it or not, for three weeks; the rain poured throughout Sunday. When we got there about one o'clock (having been invited to lunch with the Army) we found that the field kitchen had been washed out, the sergeant-cook nearly in tears, and a lot of hungry soldiers, including some very senior officers indeed. However, we three enjoyed ourselves shaking hands with old acquaintances from the late historic conflict, some now among the 'top brass', for the Doc., Jacko and myself had all served in the Corps, in some form or other. We decided, after half-an-hour, that we must set about our make-up, lunch or no lunch, and we were taken in a jeep, to our '160-lb-er', a quarter-of-a-mile away, placed reasonably near to the start of the stretcher bearing run. As the injuries were to be a large shell wound of the abdomen, and a mild fracture of the jaw, with a slight external wound of the cheek, it had been arranged previously that the Doc (who is an active casualty member of C.U. as well as medical adviser) and Jacko should be duplicates, only one casualty being required. They had been issued with a set of 'condemned' denims, as they would be badly mauled by the time we had finished with them. Webbing straps, packs, tin-hats, boots, shirts, and even identity discs, properly struck with the legend, 'Jackson, J., C. of E., 1624468', for each of them. The Doc had written a delightful letter for each to carry, purporting to come from 'Else', addressed to c/o the A.P.O. This had been given the appearance of being well-read and carried for some time, and was in each left-breast pocket. The envelope of each letter bore the usual moving inscriptions beloved by all soldiers, 'SWALK', 'ITALY', and others.

It was just as well we had foreseen the need for duplicates, though not for the reason of the wounds being disturbed, as we had thought. The abdominal wounds were made in triplicate, in case of accidents, and we used real 'guts' from a pig, a length protruding through a torn abdominal wall. The denims and shirt were torn to match, and plenty of blood poured over the whole. A small wad of blood-soaked wool was inserted in each mouth, and a small wound made on each left cheek.

The two senior judges arrived and vetted the injuries, and the Doc, now with his real identity hidden from all except the judges, beneath the bosom of Private Jackson, was to take the first run.

As Doc lay in a bit of dead ground, a W/D thunderflash went off, too near him for comfort. There was a shout of 'Stretcher bearers,' and after some minutes, a party of four arrived, with a stretcher, blankets, harness and all. By this time, the rain came down in earnest; nature provided her own thunder, without help from the Army. There was plenty of rifle fire as the bearers harnessed the casualty onto the stretcher. They then began the descent to the R.A.P. at the bottom of the ravine. From thence they had to carry to the command post, through a cleared path in the mine field, up the opposite side of the clough, and to a waiting ambulance jeep.

There were two obstacles to be negotiated, and the mine field path lay in the bed of the stream. The sides of the ravine were very steep, wooded, brambly, bushy, and extremely slippery. Rifle fire increased as the party reached the stream and more thunderflashes added to the noise of the storm. It took the first team one hour and a quarter to complete the course (the scheduled time was half-an-hour, but that had been timed the weekend previously, when the whole area was dry). Fortunately marks were not awarded for speed, but for steady progress and judicious use of cover.

Back in the tent, I was anxious about the Doc. Had the blood dried up, would the wound stand up to examination at the R.A.P. and command post, and worst of all, would he get back in time for the third team?

Jacko took the stage next, and his team took nearly an hour. By this time I had managed to get in touch, via a wireless link, with the 'base hospital' which was at the end of the course, asking them to return the Doc forthwith. They obeyed this order very promptly, even omitting to unlash him from the stretcher. The wounds were in good shape and, after a very short respite, he was ready to go out again.

Thus through five teams. After the Doc had been put ready for his last run, I parcelled up our gear and left it to be brought down by the wireless link, whilst I made the last journey with the judges, the casualty, and the bearers on the course.

Fortunately for me I was wearing a rather ancient B.R.C.S. battledress, and the Doc's service mack. My intention was to make a complete photographic record of the course . . . but down in that dim green valley with a thunderstorm overhead it was no sinecure. Nobody ever likened me to a mountain goat either, and to quote the A.D.M.S., whose help in making my descent was invaluable 'I appeared to be built for comfort rather than for speed.' He had got his boots on, and I was wearing low shoes . . . Not once, but many times, I made an undignified glissade on my stern, my uniform nylons in shreds, I had abandoned wearing my beret, my hair was dripping, and I presented a sorrier sight than the neatly trussed casualty . . .

The first obstacle was a fallen tree, hedged about with brambles, which could have been circumnavigated, but that would have taken the party into the mine field. However, the judges and I were allowed to crawl round it, and so we slopped on, through the mud and slime, and to the next obstacle, which was a collection of thorn bushes and tree trunks, which the party had to delve beneath. Then the opposite bank with fewer trees to help the ascent. The stretcher bearers took the casualty to the command post, and they dragged him up by means of ropes. The judges and I came up, hand over hand, up a rope, thoughtfully placed by the arrangers of the exercise (officers, for the use of only!). And so to the ambulance jeep, but not for any but the casualty: we had to walk back to the base. All the same, I thought for the Doc or for Jacko, a false step on the part of the stretcher bearers could have resulted in something very unpleasant, and they were powerless to help themselves.

After the marks had been totalled up, and the awards made, the A.D.M.S. made his closing remarks. He thanked the casualties, and said to the assembly that our expenses would be made from the training allowance, but the two pairs of damaged underpants (both the Doc's and Jacko's had been completely ruined by the first aiders cutting them off) would be paid for from the entertainments fund! I forebore to add that it should have been three pairs, for mine were in scarcely better shape!!

A colleague tells us — when you add generosity, understanding and loyalty to his other qualities we have a thoroughly lovable and forceful personality. Affectionately known to his fellow CUCU's as 'the little man', John Cameron Turnbull, M.R.C.S., L.R.C.P., is a bit of a Heinz — a Scot born in Bury, Lancashire, where his father was in general practice; educated at Sedburgh School; living later in Surrey and qualifying in medicine at University College, London, in 1939. Now living in Altrincham, Cheshire, where he is in partnership with two other doctors.

He served with the R.A.M.C. during the last war, seeing service at Dunkirk, in North Africa, Italy and Greece and attaining and rank of Lieut. Colonel. He is married with two children, a boy and a girl.

As a hard-working G.P. John Turnbull has little time for himself or his hobbies, but manages to do some successful colour photography and go around with his Casualties Union branch. He has been with the Altrincham branch since its inception, both as medical adviser and as a fully qualified acting member. His kindly, constructive criticism, sense of humour, keenness and enthusiasm have been of the greatest value. He is an excellent mimic and adds — when it is called for — considerable entertainment to his performance as a casualty. Epileptic fits are his *piece de resistance*, but another colleague sums up his worst casualty

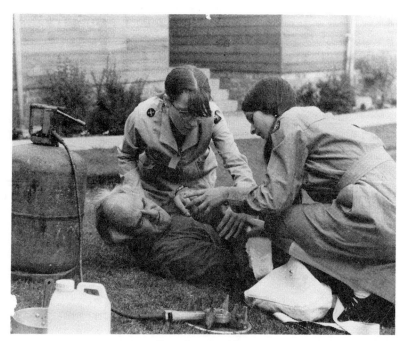

Camping troubles

experience thus:

> A casualty he fain would be,
> Reality his A.B.C.
> Flash burns and drowning were his role,
> The glory of the day he stole!
> At 'Jackson's Boat' on Mersey Banks,
> The Army lads began their pranks,
> Our hero into a pool was blown,
> Sopping and chilled right to the bone:
> The team did justice to their cause,
> And stripped their patient to his claws!

Dr. Lancelot Wills is a casualty at Stoke Mandeville Hospital.

We were invited by the hospital authorities to arrange a

casualty or casualties so that they could try out methods of handling patients with a broken neck. Lance Wills and I went along and when we arrived he insisted on being the casualty and for some couple of hours the hospital staff handled him, turning him, lifting him while applying traction, moving him by hand onto and with a stretcher. It was most interesting and I was conscious that Lance himself had enjoyed a most thrilling experience.

42

Golden Jubilee of the Orange Cross

It was with a sense of pride and gratitude that Dr. L. K. Wills and I carried greetings and good wishes from Casualties Union to *The Orange Cross* in The Hague, Holland, on the occasion of their golden jubilee. We were received with that same generous kindness I had met on my wartime visit to Holland.

We were given the opportunity of demonstrating an outline of the union technique, and we made a few interesting contacts with delegates from other countries. Eleven countries were represented. Amongst the eleven were Britons Dr. White Knox and Mr. T. E. A. Stowell. The International Jubilee Conference was held in the Kurhaus, Schreveningen, The Hague. Dr. Wills and I mounted the huge platform, large enough to accommodate a full scale orchestra and we felt very small in front of a considerable audience. The following is a reported resume of our proceedings.

On the preliminary evening Mr. E. C. Claxton and Dr. L. K. Wills gave a demonstration of Casualties Union technique to an audience of several hundred delegates and supporters from various parts of Europe. Each spoke in turn, while the other illustrated as a casualty, as follows.

CLAXTON. Ladies and gentlemen, Casualties Union is a voluntary society, which assists organizations teaching first aid, rescue and nursing by providing patients or casualties. The union was formed in 1942, and Dutch men and women volunteered for training in Eindhoven in 1944 to assist me with a programme of wartime rescue training, which as a civil engineer I had undertaken.

'It was necessary to create a sense of urgency to get the real value from rescue training. It was also necessary to choose the method of handling with regard to the injuries sustained.'

(At this stage Dr. Wills came forward, breathing with some difficulty and guarding the left side of his chest with his hands. Mr. Claxton greeted him and, pulling up a chair, suggested he would feel easier if he sat down and leant towards the injured side. Dr. Wills showed a slight easing of his distress.)

'My colleague,' continued Mr. Claxton, 'needs help. In the rescue world we learnt to carry moist cloths to wipe the face and clear the mouth from dust and debris, as we started to search for bleeding. It is the little things that count in winning the confidence and co-operation of a wounded person — things which perhaps only a casualty can know.

'Can you take a deep breath?' he asked the casualty. 'No, he cannot. With his ribs crushed, it will need care to secure him to a stretcher, before lifting him clear from wreckage.'

(Mr. Claxton slipped out of his white coat and held it like a screen between the casualty and the audience so that Dr. Wills could cease to be a casualty and slipping into the coat become the lecturer.)

WILLS. 'As a medical man teaching first aid, I need vivid illustrations for my lectures so as to leave lasting impressions with my students. I use trained casualties to illustrate my lectures upon general handling of an injured person, fractures, respiration, burns, poisons, unconsciousness, and bleeding.'

(As Dr. Wills was speaking, Mr. Claxton came forward doubled up with pain and perched on a chair. He was obviously in distress and swayed uncertainly. Before Dr. Wills could reach him, he slipped onto the floor in a faint. Rallying he exhibited the signs of abdominal haemorrhage.)

'As I explain, for example, the effects of hidden bleeding and loss of blood, the students can see for themselves the pattern that develops. The speed is increased or retarded to give time for examination and explanation. We see the thirst, the growing shortage of oxygen, the restlessness and the declining strength.'

(It was Dr. Wills turn to slip out of the white coat to rescue Mr. Claxton, who continued the commentary.)

CLAXTON. 'As a layman, I am most grateful for such memorable impressions. I recall being quite frightened, when I first saw an epileptic fit. Yet, today, no student first aider need be caught unawares, because he can see a trained casualty portray a case of epilepsy during his course of study.'

(Dr. Wills came forward looking a little strange, Suddenly, he cried out and fell unconscious. His face was contorted, his hands clenched and his back arched as he lay quite still. Suddenly he moved and began to thrash about with arms, legs and head, while blood stained froth dribbled from his lips. Meanwhile Mr. Claxton dropped on his knees to prevent him bashing his head too much and to rescue his dentures, but only got well bitten for his pains. As the convulsions subsided, the patient was gathered up in the white coat to become the speaker.)

WILLS. 'Not only has the student to learn to examine the patient, he has to learn to hold him.'

(Mr. Claxton is now lying on the floor, with his left leg overhanging the platform. Dr. Wills speaks to him but gets no reply so he lifts the patient's head and shoulders and then his arms to show that he is completely limp. The patient stirs.)

'My patient begins to come round. He has a headache and he seems conscious of his left leg. Let us examine it. There is deformity; and as one may show when lecturing on fractures, it can easily be turned into an open fracture if not firmly immobilized.'

(Suiting action to words the fracture started to bleed as the bone fragment pierced the skin. The casualty cries out and faints. Using the white coat as a screen, the casualty became the lecturer.)

CLAXTON. 'In all teaching and learning first aid the most important task is to recognize the condition of the patient. Let us do a little practice in differential diagnosis. We will take it in turns to act an injury for a few moments — you will recognize them immediately.

(Removing the white coat, he walked across the stage with some difficulty while he sorted out a recurrent displaced cartilage. From the opposite side Dr. Wills limped across with a sprained ankle. This was followed by a smashed toe, a blistered heel, intoxication,

delayed shock, broken nose, toothache, lumbago, headache, dislocated jaw, and as Dr. Wills portrayed a fractured clavicle Mr. Claxton put on the white coat and continued his remarks.)

'Each of these cases can be handled, questioned and examined to form a differential diagnosis, after which treatment can be given. In appropriate surroundings all sorts of cases can be introduced. We chose walking cases, which can be examined from afar, so that you all might see.

'Turning to treatment, the patient responds to pain, lack of confidence, insecurity, as well as to comfort and kindness. My colleague has a broken collar bone. He is unco-operative when I show diffidence and uncertainty. To a second approach, he responds quite differently and permits the injured arm to be secured immobilizing the fracture.

'Each casualty must be trained to respond to whatever treatment we may be given in the course of training, so that the student first aider may realize automatically when and where he has gone wrong.'

(The injured man having been spirited away by the white coat, Dr. Wills took over the commentary.)

WILLS. 'In the training of casualties, we have to teach them to be ill all over. There is shrinking stature, change in breathing — probably rapid and shallow, eyes lose lustre and vitality, voice is pained and distressed, movements reveal pain and loss of tone.'

(Mr. Claxton illustrated this as Dr. Wills was speaking. He started as an upright person, gradually shrinking and drooping into a battered wreck of a man.)

'In addition to this general condition, that must be kept in scale with the severity of the patient's condition, it is necessary to brief each case for special signs and symptoms and response to handling, that may be expected. We have prepared some notes for the use of our members, under the title 'ATLAS OF INJURY'. Parts I and II are available.'

(Once more released from being a casualty, Mr Claxton completed the talks.)

CLAXTON. 'We believe that the trained casualty has a valuable part to play in first aid, rescue and nursing training, bringing it to life and making it vivid. The casualty too gains unparalleled experience.

'In conclusion may we offer to The Orange Cross our

188

Dr and Mrs Oosterhuis on the canals in Amsterdam

congratulations on their jubilee and convey to them the best wishes of Casualties Union for success throughout the next fifty years.'

Back to Holland.

It was two years earlier on the occasion of the Golden Jubilee of The Orange Cross that Dr. Lancelot Wills and Eric Claxton gave a demonstration to the conference of Association Internationale de Sauvetage et de Premiers Secours en cas D'Accidents, then meeting in The Hague. During the months that followed members of The Orange Cross gave much thought to that brief demonstration and decided they wished to know more. They sent Miss F. A. Arps and Miss M. Vis to England to meet Casualties Union and attend a Civil Defence exercise at Croydon. Then came the formal invitation to the union to visit The Hague again, this time to demonstrate to the 1961 Annual General

Dr Turnbull and Eric Claxton greeted in the Hague
by Marg Vis and Dr Kesterloo

Meeting of Orange Cross.

The general management committee of Casualties Union selected their team of three and sent them off by Royal Dutch Airlines on 14th September with a tightly packed brief and orders to report back. Here they come!

We were met by Mrs. Bergmann-Kaufmann, principal secretary of Orange Cross, and Miss M. Vis who greeted us by name. 'Mrs. Nicholson, Dr. Turnbull, Mr. Claxton.' From that moment our programme was in their friendly and capable hands. And what a full programme it was! We barely had time to rehearse for our demonstration before they whisked us off to meet Dr. Kesterloo at the head offices of the Postcheque Girodienst. There we met eight of the staff who are Civil Defence instructors for the department, whom we met again the next day at The Orange Cross and a fortnight later at our own C.U. Day.

Over a pile of Casualties Union photographs we had a most animated conversation on the technique of casualty simulation, culminating with John Turnbull having one of his 'fits'. We were grateful to Dr. Kesterloo for entertaining us to lunch and some day we hope to return his hospitality.

We hastened back to our hotel to practise the make-up and complete the timing of our 'show'. Although it was pretty well streamlined already we found that make-up would have to be reduced to the barest minimum and take a very second place to acting. We found that the flushed face that goes with cerebral compression could be produced effectively by posture, by hanging the head over the edge of the platform with some muscular effort to tighten the collar. Arterial bleeding from the wrist could be shown well enough for this purpose by holding a pool of blood in the palm of the hand. Additional blood we put into a small rubber bulb concealed in a crumpled handkerchief, served for wounds and the nose bleed. Apart from these the cases were simulated by acting only.

Then came a delightful period of relaxation. We were invited in the evening to dine with the board of The Orange Cross before their annual executive meeting. We were received by the president, Dr. P. R. Michael, Professor of Surgery at Amsterdam University who set the seal upon our presence and made us feel welcome indeed in a few clever sentences in English. About thirty-four sat down to dinner, and our near neighbours shamed us by speaking fluently to us in our own language. It was a happy occasion and we liked the pattern of having one speech between each course.

When Saturday dawned we were up betimes, collected all our props and set out across the road to the Kurhaus at Scheveningen to prepare for our demonstration. We found that we had many friends among the audience whom we had met the day before. So Eric Claxton asked Mr. H. Koerts to coach him in giving a greeting to the meeting in Dutch. It sounded like double Dutch to the rest of the party but it was a valiant effort. Mr. Rijsdijk needed no second invitation to act as an interpreter for our demonstration where our acts did not explain themselves. He, and his party of first aiders supported us admirably.

We introduced ourselves as a civil engineer, a family doctor and a housewife and showed what Casualties Union technique can do for first aid in the hands of those who understand it.

Professor Michael

We showed how bandaging practice could be improved by using trained patients, and how the practising of treatments could be made so much more realistic by having skilled, made-up casualties to show the injuries, and also to say what the treatment felt like.

Dr. Turnbull then gave a series of casualties that he would use when lecturing on haemorrhage. Eric Claxton and Helen Nicholson produced seven cases for him graded from a cut knee to a severe internal haemorrhage requiring a transfusion of blood. They appeared and reappeared from behind a screen where the make-up and the small props were concealed.

Helen Nicholson gave a session on the way we stage a diagnosis exercise, and all three took it in turns to be the casualty or do the diagnosis by questioning and handling. For these we needed no make-up for we gave them an epileptic fit, a diabetic collapse, heart attack, and fractures of the femur, pelvis and spine. the audience got them all right!

The accident we staged in front of the audience to show how it was planned, using a table lamp for the electric

Dr J.A. Molhuyson

shock and a photograph apparatus for the flash. Then we sat on the platform and reminisced about our experiences when acting as casualties, and we could have gone on all day, but our hour and a quarter was up.

In proposing a vote of thanks Professor Michael demonstrated the behaviour of a traveller suddenly taken ill on a long train journey, and asked Helen Nicholson what she would do. She just fainted! The audience liked that and we presented the president with the badge of the union for his own performance.

We also offered the badge of the union to Dr. J. A. Molhuysen, an octogenarian, who is engaged in writing a new first aid handbook.

After the tense, high-pitched activity of our demonstration we were glad to cool down and relax over lunch with Mr. J. H. Schuller tot Peursum, treasurer to The Orange Cross and Rear Admiral Dr. W. A. Borgeld, head medical officer of the Dutch Red Cross.

Our Programme included several other delights, not least of which was a tour of lovely parts of Holland with Dr. and Mrs. Oosterhuis as our hosts. We parted with many

A welcome from Dr and Mrs Oosterhuis with
Mrs Bergman Kaufmann and a Lady from Volendam

expressions of hope on both sides of more exchange visits.

Dr. and Mrs. Oosterhuis pay Casualties Union a return visit

To our great delight the secretary general of the Association
Internationale de Sauvetage et de Premier Secours en cas
d'Accidents, Dr. Oosterhuis and his wife, became our guests
of honour on Casualties Union Day in 1961, when the
union was guest of the R.A.F. at their Stanmore Depot. Dr.
Oosterhuis addressed the gathering with much warmth.
'Almost a year ago I received, in my quality as secretary
general of the International Association, your kind invitation
to attend your Casualties Union Day. I am very thankful
because I think that herewith is shown the international
importance of Casualties Union.

'In my function as a secretary of the Royal Dutch Society
of The Orange Cross, I had the privilege of seeing the
wonderful demonstration given by Mrs. Nicholson, Dr.
Turnbull and Mr. Claxton during our annual meeting at
The Hague. The enthusiasm was so great that five of our

Dr and Mrs Oosterhuis welcomed by Dr and Mrs Glyn Hughes
at the Rugby Football ground at Twickenham

best instructors are here today, to catch the trick from you.
We hope to start courses in our country on the level of your
work, and we will gladly avail ourselves of the help and
advice you so kindly offered. We hope to be good pupils.

'In our small country, where we also occupy ourselves
intensively with first aid, we started grease painting patients
for our competitions, but now we know there is more to be
done. It is of the utmost importance that the patients also
know how they have to act.

'Knowing how much there is to be done to make such a
day a success, I admire immensely what I have seen here
today, and I believe that it can contribute to furthering the
idea of first aid and fraternisation. I hope that representatives of Casualties Union can attend our next International
Congress in Zurich in September, 1962.

'My wife and I are very thankful for the hearty reception
accorded to us. It is a great pleasure to be 'at home' in so
short a time. Thank you very much indeed. I wish

Dr Oosterhuis presents the Lotus Trophy to Casualties Union

Casualties Union may continue this wonderful work for the benefit of mankind.'

In my 'commentary' following that enjoyable occasion I observed that we had been greatly stimulated and encouraged by the visit of Dr. and Mrs. Oosterhuis who came from Holland to be our guests of honour on C.U. Day. We were charmed by their company and delighted by the warmth and enthusiasm with which they studied the demonstrations

Mary Jacobs receives the Lotus Trophy from Colonel Kneepkins

and competitions. It was an equal joy for me to go to The Hague as the guest of The Orange Cross, to talk about and demonstrate C.U. technique and how it can be used to make training more vivid. We made many interesting contacts with a wide representation of first aid organizations in Holland.

43

Twenty-First Anniversary

Once more I would like to quote from my 'commentary' at that time —

'Friday, 22nd November, 1963 is the twenty-first anniversary of Casualties Union and marks the completion of the first stage in the development of this independent body. It has been a period of great changes in the history of mankind. The attitude of mind has been changed by the introduction of health and social services, with its consequent shifting of responsibility from the individual to the community. The service of members has I believe made some contribution to the maintenance of personal responsibility of one human being for his fellow; a purpose in which each individual retains absolute dignity and integrity.

'Casualties Union was formed because the people who studied the behaviour of sick and injured people and endeavoured to portray that behaviour learnt more by feeling what handling and treatment were like than has ever been written in first aid books. It gave the whole proceedings a new vigour. Now with twenty-one years of experience from the revealing point of view of the casualty, the union unhesitatingly invites members of all organizations to share this revealing experience. It would emphasise the importance of studying the behaviour of sick and injured persons and their response to approach, handling and treatment of one kind or another.

'No one of us remains unaffected by the inspiration

engendered by this work and the outstanding people who have served its cause. I have been greatly inspired by the splendid men who have been our president. Each of them was an outstanding leader in his own field — W. P. Robinson, C.B.E., M.I.C.E., Brigadier W. Rowley Bristow, C.B.E., D.S.O., M.C., F.R.C.S., St. J. D. Buxton, F.R.C.S., Major-General P. H. Mitchiner, C.B., C.B.E., F.R.C.S., T.D., Brigadier H. L. Glyn Hughes, C.B.E., D.S.O., M.C., M.R.C.S.

'Having broken away on this auspicious occasion from my habit of keeping these notes impersonal, I am tempted to refer by name to some others whose service has inspired me. I realize that in making reference to some I must inevitably leave out perhaps three times as many who are just as deserving of mention. To them I send my best wishes as well as my gratitude. Your service is every bit as important.

'The names that come especially to my mind: Edward Akester, Brenda Whiteley, Bill Warn, Dr. James Barford, Eric Buchler, L. D. Doelberg, Sambo, Edith Winsloe, Robin Young, R. Cortazzi, Roy Stokes, Dr. M. M. Pam, Doris Hammer, John Stevens, Pat and John Loarridge, Col. Edward Goss, and Dr. W. C. Bentall in the wartime development; later in the most difficult striving for peace, others join them: Harry Davies, Nancy Budgett, Amy Adie, Helen Nicholson, Steve Eaton, Fred Yearron, John Wise, M. McCarthy, Dr. J. Edgar Haine, Dr. L. S. Michaelis, Ina Robb, Mary Macmillan, Gib, Dr. L. A. Eastwood, Doris Hancox, Theo Behrens, Barry Blix, Dr. L. K. Wills, Nell McLintock, Arthur Ferris, Aileen Poulton, Dr. John Turnbull, Cyril Wallis, Harry Excell, Peter Pendry, Dr. John Binning, Kay Bowring, Dr. Colin Dawson, Dr. A. Gordon, M. E. Philbrick, Dr. J. Watson, R. J. Dymond. Each name brings back memories as each and every one of them added his contribution to the mosaic that is Casualties Union. Not perhaps upon paper but in fellowship and brotherhood/sisterhood, which is the essence of our cause.

'Reassurance is a word that has been used many times in every treatise on first aid. It is, however, a word that takes on a new meaning when one experiences comfort of care, kindness and expert gentleness. It becomes even more significant in its absence when called upon to respond to

Senior Instructor Alwyn Law and her husband Fred who was a Chemist
and a most helpful helper member

cursory indifference at the all too common hand of
ignorance. In our humble role as 'casualty' we have realized
the enormous power for good created by sincere sympathy
and kindness, gentleness and that sense of security conveyed
by skilled hands — doctor's, nurse's, or first aider's.

'It is therefore a matter of special interest to note the
emphasis being placed upon attention to morale by the
American medical world. No doubt similar thoughts were
behind the comments of Sir George Pickering in his
presidential address to the British Medical Association when
he said,

'. . . it is human sympathy and understanding
that form the very core of medicine.'

'I believe that a first aider can give such confidence to his
patients that the rot of disaster is immediately stemmed and
the fight back to health started by constructive goodwill,
gentle firmness and genuine sympathy.

'There is no better way of coming face to face with the
need for developing such an attitude of mind than in the

200

role of "casualty", once one has been trained to be receptive ... What can you do to help? Build up the morale and with it the aim for higher standard and these will gradually generate themselves.

'In the years to come, may we all be constructive and generous in our comments, yet determined to develop the highest sense of morale and service, as well as the highest possible standard of realism and its application to all types of training and study. NEVER WAS THERE GREATER NEED OR OPPORTUNITY.'

44

Anniversary Dinner at the Royal College of Surgeons

What a joy to be invited to celebrate once more in these august surroundings. But let the members speak for themselves by this symposium.

FROM THE TOP TABLE

It was a great joy, a thrill, a wonderful experience to enrich the memory, a highlight of friendship and dedication; it was certainly all these things. But above all it was a manifestation of the living spirit of an inspired idea which has brought men and women of all classes and callings together to serve their fellow men by taking their places in accident situations and distressful conditions, that they might not suffer so much in the future.

The venue itself implied an acceptance of Casualties Union in the brotherhood of the healing skills. The Royal College of Surgeons has seen many distinguished gatherings, but this one was distinguished by the sincere affection in which this movement has bound each to its founder and to each other. Coal miners and hospital matrons, police constables and professors sat down together with accountants and ambulance drivers, surgeons and secretaries, to enjoy refreshment for body, mind and spirit. The great surgeons of the past looked down benignly on many for whom this provided poignant memories and on all of us who were dedicating our services to the future.

FROM A FOUNDER MEMBER

When I first received the invitation to the dinner I refused
— I am not fond of functions — it was too far to go — too
great an effort — it was all so long ago. Then a friend
suggested a joint venture. We went — and am I glad we
did!

Frankly, I was overwhelemed with the scale, scope and
vigour of the modern Casualties Union. The baby born
twenty-one years ago had been a lively, promising youngster,
but that it would have grown into *this* and so *respectable!* We
originals were an awful lot of ruffians as I remember.

It was good to recognize many familiar faces, less changed
than I expected; but sobering to hear how many of our old
colleagues had died in the intervening years. Those early
days were a wonderful experience. Probably our efforts
would seem pretty crude in the light of modern techniques,
but we felt we were standing in for real casualties, which
were occurring with such appalling frequency. The special
tensions of war conditions gave us stimulus; it takes different
qualities to continue the work at the lower emotional level
of peace time, and I feel a great admiration for those who
have persevered and developed C.U. to its present stage. It
is undoubtedly important work and I wish it continued
success.

FROM A NEW MEMBER

Entering the Royal College of Surgeons with its impressive
atmosphere produced among us a feeling of awe and
reverence for the great tradition it enshrined. We felt very
small fry in a new organization until we realized the honour
that was being paid us by being there at all. We were on
the brink of acceptance by the medical world.

Being received by our president and his wife and then
being welcomed into a room full of chattering CUCU's
where we exchanged experiences with members old and new

from far and near, made us feel at once part of the spirit which is Casualties Union.

As course followed course, and happy conversation flowed freely round the tables, we felt reluctant to stop and listen to several boring speeches. But what a wonderful surprise to find that contrary to the usual, they were most enlightening and entertaining. We were astonished to see the time when the last speaker sat down. It was a great thrill for us, a whole study circle of new members from the east midlands, to be part of this inspiring gathering.

The celebration dinner held at the Royal College of Surgeons of England in the Lumley Hall was an inspiration. It was graced by some of our earliest members and by others from all over the United Kingdom who had been admitted to membership a little more recently. Well over a hundred and fifty sat down to dine. There were some inspiring speeches in the mellow aftermath of a delightful meal and the evening was over far too quickly.

Earlier in the evening just before dinner, an opportunity was made to present a testimonial to Percy Sargeant at a little ceremony conducted by Dr. Lancelot Wills in the presence of the whole company. To our great pleasure Mrs. Sargeant was present to we were able to express our thanks to them both.

And so ended a remarkable and wonderful evening among beautiful people in a delightful environment. But this was not the end of our celebrations because we were about to publish a splendidly illustrated souvenir entitled *Twenty-One Years in Your Hands*. It contained tributes from the Minister of Health, the Rt. Hon. Enoch Powell; and senior representatives of all the important organizations that we serve.

TOAST LIST
GRACE

☆ ☆ ☆

HER MAJESTY THE QUEEN

☆ ☆ ☆

ABSENT FRIENDS
Remembered by Mrs. (Brenda) Whiteley

☆ ☆ ☆

21 YEARS AS UNDERSTUDY
TO THE VICTIMS OF TOMORROW
Proposed by Dr. J. Edgar Haine, M.B., B.Ch., D.P.H.P.
Reply by Eric Claxton, M.B.E., B.Sc., M.I.C.E.,

☆ ☆ ☆

THE EMERGENCY SERVICES IN PEACE AND WAR
Proposed by Mrs. Helen M. Nicholson
Reply by Col. John Watts, O.B.E., M.C., M.B., F.R.C.S.

☆ ☆ ☆

THE GUESTS
Proposed by the President
Reply by
Sir George Godber, C.B., M.D., F.R.C.P., D.P.H.

45

A Message From The President

Once again I have the opportunity to send you all seasonal greetings, good wishes and profound gratitude to one and all for the enthusiasm and unselfish devotion which has been put into your efforts for Casualties Union during the past year.

We are now rapidly approaching our coming of age and I think can justifiably look back with pride on our achievements during the past twenty years. Our organization has gone from strength to strength and, in addition to its recognition by the various government departments and national bodies, has achieved an international reputation. This was very evident on C.U. day when, for the first time entries for our competition came from abroad, and our guest of honour came from Holland to honour our function.

Our annual day seems to get better and the standards higher. It is thanks to you that it is so. It is always a wonderful reunion and a chance to renew old friendships and make new ones. It is also a stimulus to our efforts which in the present unsettled state of the world and the many areas of active strife, become of increasing importance.

I would like to end by saying thank you once again to Eric Claxton for the birth of this movement, and to every member of Casualties Union for your continuing effort. Let us help to make this Christmas a time of peace and goodwill.

H. L. GLYN HUGHES

46

Why Is An Accident?

H.R.H. Prince Philip told the assembled company at the Royal College of Surgeons that he had kept his fingers crossed all the way coming through London in his car. He was addressing the Convention on Accident Prevention and Life Saving called by the Royal College on 14th and 15th May, 1963. In saying that while the scourge of disease is being lifted the new scourge of accidents is taking its place, H.R.H. made a poignant statement on the irresponsible attitude to the safety of others engendered by the changing social pattern. As the champion of the adventurous spirit of youth, the Duke held forth strongly in favour of adequate training to take calculated risks, and negatived the so-called toughness ascribed to nitwits who barge about making things dangerous for other people.

Crash! And attention was momentarily deflected from the royal visitor as Sir Arthur Porritt conducted him round the exhibition stalls. The Duke was quick to see the point of the demonstration staged by Casualties Union. Joan Brackin played the part of a waitress who had stumbled with her tray of empty tea cups. Broken crocks scattered amongst surrounding feet and the cost of her fractured ankle to the individual, to her employers and to the health services, was made clear by our commentator. It was no accident, it was caused by her wearing a pair of ill-fitting shoes with stiletto heels, quite unsuitable for her job.

Much time was taken up at the convention by speakers

Prince Phillip visits the Royal College of Surgeons
and meets casualty Joan Brackin

quoting statistics. Surely these are readily available to anyone who remains unconvinced that we have an enormous problem on our hands? Less readily available was a really constructive contribution to the task of lessening careless behaviour which leads to personal damage and death. To anyone who has studied accident causation sufficiently well to stage mishaps in accurate detail, the effects are very apparent. An accident is hardly ever a thing of chance, but is inevitable. Something is left lying about on the floor and somebody falls over it. You stand on an unsteady perch and the odds are you will tumble off it. A vehicle driven with no regard for the rules is a menace on the roads. But don't blame the vehicle — blame the driver. Mishaps anywhere don't just happen — they are caused.

People are the cause of accidents, and prevention is a matter of education, not of legislation. Until people are rendered sensitive to the safety of themselves and of others, statistics for injuries and death will continue to appal.

People could be taught to be safety conscious as soon as they can read, if educationalists really cared whether their charges were going to live long enough to benefit from their education. It would amount to educating a sixth sense, that of awareness. Coupled with unselfishness, this could have effects far outreaching the aim of reducing the amount of personal damage now being caused by thoughtlessness. It is the answer to more than accident prevention because it has *positive* value.

No trained member of Casualties Union could leave a banana skin lying on the pavement, or meddle with electric wires while the current is on. There seems to be a clue to the remedy here.

47

Other People's Shoes

'If I were in your shoes, I wouldn't have any trouble from my mother-in-law.' Oh! Wouldn't you? Really? You know, if you were in that person's shoes, you'd be another person and much closer to a complex situation.

Surely there we have two keys to the success of undertaking the kind of acting required of Casualties Union members. Being *another person,* and being *closer to the situation.*

We have no footlights or soft music to help us overcome our self-consciousness. Our audience not only sees and hears us but they are close at hand and can touch us. We cannot resort to acting in the usual sense of the word, or depend on glamour or heroics to see us through. Very often we are at our best when silent and look our worst. The achievement of the kind of acting required of a trained casualty depends on the ability to change one's mental atmosphere. It means both mentally and to a large extent physically, transplanting oneself into someone else's shoes.

The idea of trying to teach acting in this way came to me when I was producing an incident for a competition in the assembly hall of a school. The accident was given every semblance of reality by using step-ladders, planks and buckets, and by dressing our casualties as cleaners. I had briefed a member to act a dislocated shoulder, and was sure he could do it faultlessly.

But before the competition had been underway for two minutes, I was consumed with mental agony. I heard coming from the platform a very top drawer, affected voice saying, 'Oh, dear! Please don't touch my arm, it is so painful.' Of course, I had not made sure he could speak the language of my friends, the cleaners, that warm, rich lingo of the floor cloth and mop jungle. It was such a good dislocated shoulder, absolutely ruined by the lack of the true atmosphere and character in which it happened. He was still wearing his own shoes! The more I think of it, the more I am convinced that one simply cannot act *just* an injury. One must become identified with a person in a given situation first and add the injury afterwards. It means getting into the shoes of the real casualty.

Shoes are fascinating things. They are much more necessary and interesting than hats! Watch the shoes of the passers-by next time you wait for a bus. Study the shoes opposite you in the train. To the keen observer, shoes go a long way towards guessing occupation, and with a little help from the rest of the apparel they complete an impression of personality and even character. In fairy tale land they play a high part in determining destiny, if you recall the fate of the wearer of the glass slippers and of the red shoes.

I knew of an old man who lived in London who made shoes and practised as a herbalist. People would tell him of their complaints and he would ask them to bring him one of their well worn shoes. By observing the strains and tread he came very close to a complete diagnosis for the wearer. A rare gift of perception — sincerely used.

There is much to be learned from the symbolism of standing in someone else's shoes. Here is a method of teaching acting which may stimulate the imagination of the shy, reserved student to venture beyond the limited field of his own interpretation of any particular injury. Make-up of the mind should play as much a part in the briefing of a casualty as the make-up of the skin. We are not always called upon to be casualties in circumstances in which we ourselves would be found. I found it both interesting and thrilling to be a casualty caught up in a capstan lathe, a world of which I knew nothing until that episode. The miner takes the place of the farm hand, and the ambulance driver stands in for the bank manager. It is very refreshing,

Newcastle Branch wins the Lotus Trophy

Photo by courtesy of Mobile Photo Service, Gateshead

but they all wear different shoes.

Sometimes when you have enjoyed a film or a play very much and you have identified yourself with a character in it that has caught your imagination, you can recall a sense of being a different person for some time afterwards. You have really thought yourself into the personality you have admired. Though you may bear no resemblance to Peter O'Toole or Brigitte Bardot, you tend to think in their terms, and half expect people to notice how dashing or how slim you really are!

It should be possible to employ much the same thought processes for our purpose of absorbing a briefing, spoken or written. Our medical advisers may have something to say about the dangers of thinking oneself into injury conditions, but there is surely no comparison between this type of identification and the result of neurosis or anxiety state when the functional disorder may seem to have no connection at all with conscious thought.

Here is an exercise which instructors could try in their acting sessions. It needs a miscellaneous collection of footwear such as sandals and old carpet slippers, city shoes and winkle-pickers, knavvies' boots and sports shoes, stilettos and clogs. Ask your students to imagine the various owners as they have stood in them when they have been hurt or happy, sad or gay. Select an injury, such as a sprained ankle, and ask the students to stand in each pair of shoes in turn and interpret the same injury from inside the mind of the likely owner of each pair. There should be a fascinating difference between the debutante who sprains her ankle at her 'coming-out ball' and the stevedore who treads clumsily on a coil of rope.

Played as a game, the exercise will be useful in developing the disciplined mental approach so necessary to our type of acting. Considered as a philosophical exercise it might go far towards helping us to understand other people's point of view (without necessarily agreeing with it). For understanding leads to sympathy, and sympathy to kindness. And kindness is the greater part of living and takes the fear out of dying.

HELEN M. NICHOLSON

48

Acting As A Casualty
An Interview with Brenda Whiteley

ACTING — BEHAVIOUR — CONDUCT — EXPRES-
SION — RESPONSE — EMOTION — REACTION — a
person behaves differently, when he is happy compared with
when he is miserable, unwell, anxious, afraid, or hopeless as
the accompanying photographs indicate. There is a great
change in the eyes, in the mouth, in the brow, in the
cheeks, in the nose and in the jaw.

There is no doubt that the photographs tell their story;
yet all were taken quickly, one after another. Such discipline
and skill is typical of our talented and experienced Vice-
President, Mrs. R. F. (Brenda) Whiteley.

I asked her to give some advice to help beginners. 'Live
the part,' she replied. 'Think yourself into it, talking to give
you the atmosphere. Do not falter; even if you think you
have spoilt your act, go on with it. It is the sincerity with
which you play the part that gets over. Feel the disability,
the pain, the fear, the weakness, and you will show it.'

Brenda carried herself into each part by speaking words
appropriate to the condition and situation. As soon as we
paused to adjust the camera, I dived in with another
question. 'When you are going to act as a casualty, how do
you prepare?'

'By working myself deliberately into the part. First I put
on appropriate clothing. This helps me to realize what I was
doing immediately beforehand, and helps me to appreciate

| ENDURANCE | HORROR | PAIN |

| AIR HUNGER | SHOCK | ANXIETY |

Brenda Whiteley enacts various emotions

the accident or casualty situation. The situation is developed further in the details of disarray of clothing, dirty marks, the blouse pulled loose at the waist or the undone button. Damage to my clothing emphasises the pattern of what happened and I become part of it.'

'What next?' I prompted.

'Make-up. As I prepare my face, I become aware of just how ill I am. The make-up of injuries emphasises the location of damage and pinpoints the areas of acute pain.'

'Anything else?'

'Lots more. The environment and my personal position make me conscious of the horror of the situation and the discomfort and the fear of further injury. It makes me appreciate the situation of any other casualty or person involved.' After a pause she continued, 'Words must be found that are appropriate to the injury and to the cause. Words help to create the emotion, which reveals the full implication of the situation; for myself; for others involved or in any way affected — my family, my work or my friends.'

'Which is the most important?' I asked.

'To the nurse, rescuer or first aider, who will handle the situation, the behaviour is most important, but the situation may determine the methods they must adopt and sets the limitations. The make-up and my position in the setting and the others involved are a great help to me in acting.'

'How does this help?'

'These suggest words and phrases to me, which in turn help me to develop the emotions.'

'Would you say that the portrayal of the emotions was an important feature?'

'Certainly. It is, I think, the part that finally convinces those who handle you, that you are in need of assistance.'

'Do you find that words help greatly to put over the changing emotions?'

'Yes. I find that speaking emphasises the slight differences in breathing, vitality, weakness, and enables one to create expressions — calm, joy, fun, concern, anxiety, endurance, courage, horror and so on.'

'Have you any special phrases that help you to concentrate upon a particular emotion?'

'Not really, I think. They seem to go together and they embrace the situation as well. Let us try a few.'

CALM: 'Help the others first. Don't worry about me. I can wait.'

RELIEF: 'Thank God, he is all right.'

FUN: 'This really is funny. Just the sort of thing I would do. I ought to have known better — one of my off-days.'

CONCERN: 'I hope he'll be all right. Is he badly hurt?' Alternatively, 'How soon, d'you think, I can get back to work?' It depends on the situation.

ANXIETY: 'I feel so ill. Am I going to die?' Or, perhaps, 'Be careful how you handle him; don't make it worse.'

ALARM: 'Look out. It's catching fire.'

HORROR: 'Oh, my God, no. No. NO. IT MUSTN'T. STOP IT.'

SURPRISE: 'It's YOU. How wonderful.'

PAIN: 'I'm alright; it hurts a bit . . . yes, it's pretty bad, but I can stick it . . . it shoots all the way up . . . I can't bear it much longer . . .'

SHOCK: '. . . it . . . all . . . happened . . . so . . . quickly . . .' (Voice feeble: long pauses while understanding or grasping the question and slow reply.)

WEAKNESS: 'I can't go on . . . I feel awful . . . Can you help me? . . .'

AIR-HUNGER: Gulps at air and no speech is possible.

NAUSEA: 'Burp . . . I feel sick . . . I am going to be sick — QUICK.'

COURAGE: 'Tell me when it is going to hurt.'

ENDURANCE: 'It's all right. I can stick it. Don't be longer than you can help.'

LOSS OF NERVE: 'Don't leave me . . . Stay with me . . .'

As we spoke these words, I felt transported from one emotion to another. 'Do words help you in other ways?' I asked.

'Yes,' replied Brenda, 'they help to pinpoint the injury and are essential for indicating the symptoms.'

'Finally is there any special advice you would care to give on the portrayal of a casualty?'

'Get away quietly by yourself — away from the chatter of the make-up room — to think yourself into the part. The more experienced people try to get away for at least five minutes. I prefer ten minutes. I needed longer still at first.'

I noticed that Brenda couldn't help using her hands to express each reaction and emotion. As her facial expression changed, so her hands made a complimentary gesture, such as clasping each other, grasping the chair for steadiness, gripping her clothing to express pain, stroking her face to smooth away an ache. Even her feet were busy changing her position to show restlessness, tension, fear or weakness. She had thought herself so completely into the part that no essential movement was lacking or wasted. I was more than ever convinced that great acting needs great thinking.

49

The Red Thread
A Study in Casualty Responsibility

As soon as somebody is hurt and there is anyone within eye or ear-shot, a tie is created which only time can break. Whether you react positively by helping, or negatively by going away, you become emotionally and physically involved in the situation.

Imagine that you are passing along a street in a bus, an elderly man steps off the pavement and is knocked down by a passing cyclist. As you look back you see the old man raise his face, streaming with blood, from the edge of the pavement. At once a host of relationships spring into being. You feel for the old man, and for the cyclist. Both emotional relationships but very real. You feel quite sick and cold. You wish you could do something to help, or you are glad you are on a bus which is not stopping. The scene is printed in your mind's eye, your hands begin to sweat and you rub them together in an unconscious effort to wash your hands of the incident. But it won't go away. It remains with you throughout the rest of the day. As you begin to fall asleep that night a kaleidoscope of the day shakes up the pattern and you are awakened with a jerk as your dream shows you one of your own children fall from a bicycle in front of your bus. It takes the rest of the week to get the incident into proportion.

Your sensitivity to old men stepping off pavements near passing bicycles lasts subconsciously for a lifetime. And you only *saw* it, you didn't *hear* it or *feel* the situation through handling the old man like your friend who was ten feet away from him when it happened.

Your friend did not feel sick. His relationship with the old man was different from yours. It was physical. He was able to do something about it, and worked off the emotional upset through his hands, his voice, taking off his coat to lay under the old man's head, dabbing the blood away that was running into his eyes. He held the old man's hand until the ambulance came. He was sick afterwards.

The old man in his plight had unwittingly created as many relationships as there were people who saw him lying there. There was a red thread stretched between him and every individual in that short but busy street; to those who could not bear the sight of blood and hurried away; to those who 'love a good accident' and form the inevitable crowd. Even to the hard-headed playboy on the other side of the street, who said to his girl, 'Oh, just another old guy gone for a burton.' The girl felt different. It might have been her father.

The red threads were all taut because the old man's plight was so real. It stirred the emotions of each observer. It made some cold, some cry, some bite their nails, some hurry away. In those best placed to help him, it summoned up the best efforts of first aid of which they had ever been aware. And it wasn't just the quantity of blood upon the face; it was the awkward way he was lying in the gutter, his pension book still clutched in his hand, his ragged cap flung ten feet away among the feet of the passers-by, one knee cut through a torn trouser leg. It was his feebleness and his groans that kept the tension on the threads.

Your task as a stand-in casualty is to make and keep the tension on the threads. Each time you go into action as a casualty, the strands to make up the threads are put into your hands. They are history, staging, acting, reacting, make-up and timing, which twisted together, have so much more tensile strength than any one of them alone. You hold the threads taut by concentration, sincerity, a sense of purpose and the ability to identify yourself with the circumstances of the casualty whose place you are taking.

You have to create the relationship between casualty and

first aider, firstly by the reality of the situation shown in the staging, then by the sincerity of acting. Make-up comes a good third, but it only adds to the emotional atmosphere and it is a guide to diagnosis.

Having created the relationship you must hold it at the effective tension — much in the way that a singer, or an instrumentalist, or an actor holds an audience; just as an artist communicates to you through his picture, or a friend through the great art of letter writing. The art is in keeping the tension just right.

There are times when attention is focussed on another character in the situation, and there occurs an opportunity of resting before one becomes the centre of activity once more; even then the red thread must be kept taut by behaving in pattern. Watch any great actor from whom the limelight is withdrawn, quietly playing the part on the fringe without drawing attention to himself, and yet fully aware that he is part of the picture, and that some eyes are sure to be upon him. So it is with the casualty for whom a waiting period occurs, perhaps between treatment and transport. Training and experience add up to a convincing performance even in the shadows of the stage, for the red thread stretches to the perimeter and beyond. You have to play to the people in the wings as well, otherwise you weaken your own concentration.

Interpreted in terms of casualty acting it means taking your part seriously from the moment you leave the make-up room until you return to it. There is disaster in smiling and joking with the judges or the audience in competition work when the first aider turns his back for a moment or before he leaves the stage. You will have snapped the red thread.

Make it your responsibility to create the atmosphere or urgency intrinsic to accident situations, by the integrity of your behaviour from start to finish. You may not be responsible for the staging, which may be a mockery of reality; or the make-up which was done too hurriedly; but the high sense of purpose in your acting may save a whole event from being a travesty.

Once you have taken the red threads into your hands, think of them as being the life blood of a real casualty.

HELEN M. NICHOLSON

50

The Eloquence of Hands

*Do you use your hands to support the thoughts and words
with which you express the signs and symptoms of injury?*

Spontaneously, you wave to your friends in greeting or
farewell. The action seems to be the same, yet what a
different feeling it conveys. In contrast, the hostile make
equally eloquent gestures by the shaking of their fists.

These gestures create an atmosphere, as the message they
convey is given and received. Their meaning is clear. The
mood and tone — the affection, the sorrow, the familiarity,
the novelty, the excitement, the enthusiasm, the sincerity,
the hostility, the ruthlessness — is expressed and understood.
Not only the broad gesture is conveyed but the shade of
mood as well.

Coming closer, the hand outstretched in greeting tells
without the need for words, the joy, or the misery of the
moment. Clasping hands express courage, power, health,
hope, weakness or desperation to each other. So eloquent
can be the hands that lovers will sit in ecstasy for hours
with fingers intertwined. But this involves the power of
touch.

Just watch the hands of anyone, anywhere, at any time.
Immediately you know a great deal about the owner. You
see his confidence or nervousness, his delight, his boredom,
his peacefulness, fear or distress. You can measure nervous
tension by watching hands. They play a continuous role

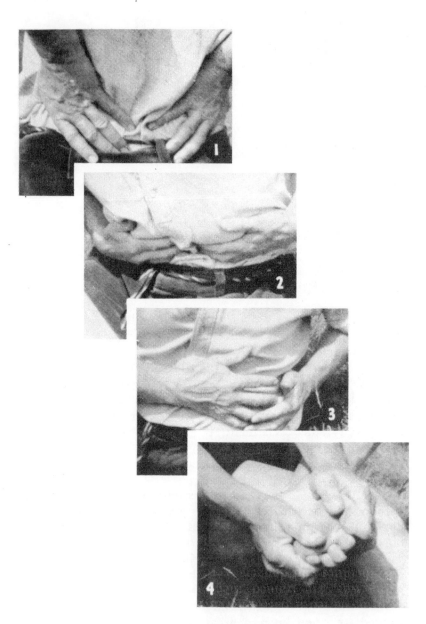

The Eloquence of Hands, 1 to 4

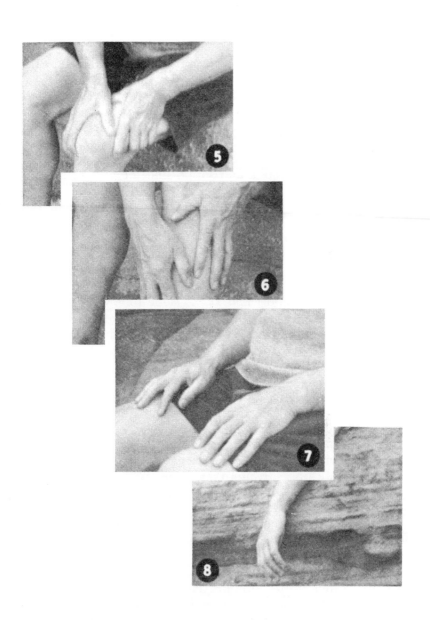

The Eloquence of Hands, 5 to 8

recording for others to see the emotion of our life. Even in sleep or unconsciousness, they play their consistent and expressive part.

The message of the hands tell the doctor and the skilled first aider the true condition of the most spartan casualty. They can tell when he has pain, where the pain is and the sort of pain.

Stricken with lumbago, the hands go to the small of the back, splinting, warming and supporting the area of painful muscular spasm (1). The climber, winded by a fall, holds firmly, even perhaps energetically, the painful area of the solar plexus (2). Hands guarding the injured part do not necessarily touch the injury, but provide a protective cage, some slight warmth perhaps, a clear indication of the quality of the pain and its whereabouts, and the apprehension of the victim in his fear of further injury (3). The sensitive fingers support and at the same time search for the exact location of the pain and the severity of the injury. This generally indicates less severe damage or more deeply seated pain (4).

Intense pain in the knee is clearly shown by the tightly gripping it with both hands so that the fingers show white tips through the nails, as they attempt to stifle the pain (5). In contrast the soothing warmth and comfort of the hands which ease the pain of the bruised shin (6).

Every injury and every condition has its appropriate hand behaviour, which is in keeping with the casualty's temperament and surroundings. They tell so much that when deliberately not used their 'silence' tells a different story — the peaceful relaxed picture of unemotional restfulness (7), or the limp hand hanging over the rocks leading without mistake to the unconscious wanderer who having lost his footing above has fallen to the rocky ledge (8).

Watch other people's hands. Notice how they mirror the mood, character, calling and environment of their owner. Then when you are acting as a casualty, use your hands to express distress, pain, loss of function, fear, frustration, courage, with their eloquence in support of your voice and facial expression in portraying every injury. It will present a truer picture to those who handle you and give you confidence to drop without strain right into the part.

The power of communication through the hands could be the subject of a whole article. Suffice it to say here that trained casualties can convey their feelings of pain and distress, fear and weakness in the way they take hold of the first aider's hands or clothing. Through your hands you will say so much of value in diagnosis, leading the first aider to give of his best in helpful treatment. Make this contribution by your skilled acting and you will have done untold teaching by creating a relationship between yourself and whoever comes to your aid.

ERIC CLAXTON

Doctor Plays The Harp
Reluctant hero gets practice on Christmas Eve

Doctors are seldom good patients, but on one occasion I was horrified to find a doctor friend of mine flat out under what was left of a grand piano. I was powerless to help. My job was to take photographs. Doc looked frightfully ill and suffered terribly during the agonizing wait while someone was called to do something about it. He'd been playing himself a tune, when the big bang had done its worst. He was stretched out on a pile of rubble with the frame of the piano across his middle. The whole was kept firmly in place by the roof which had settled down on top of the lot.

Doc was not aware of the bang, nor the landing on the rubble, for he was stunned for a while. He came too feeling very cold round his shoulders. As he tried to move to discover where he was and what had happened, a great pain stabbed him in his middle somewhere below his hips and he fainted.

When he came to for the second time, his wandering fingers struck the strings on the piano frame and he had the sensation of awakening in heaven. Courageously he plucked at the chords and a shower of plaster dust fell onto his face. He was conscious of sharp points digging into his back, seat and legs, but the sharpest pains were somewhere in the lower region of his abdomen. Apart from the pain, when he tried to move either his body or legs, he felt a most distressing lack of security, as though he was no longer

Doctor plays the harp

properly tied together. Perhaps this was part of the shedding of the body.

Between oblivion he twanged subconsciously at his harp and knocked his elbow hard against some massive brick rubble releasing another shower of dust. It was this in all probability that more than anything brought him back to consciousness. He was dry and his teeth were gritty from the dust. He tried to move, but found he was securely fixed across his middle. He called for help, but no-one came. He fell to plucking the chords again and found that he could make a tune. Part dream, part waking, he remained suspended between heaven and earth.

There is no doubt that his playing attracted attention when wardens and rescuemen appeared on the scene. With great difficulty and not a little pain he was released, placed upon a door and put into the first available ambulance. The easing of the pain convinced him that he had now escaped from his body.

His next door neighbour was trapped by the same roof.

227

He could not move because of the pain in his back and because, in spite of his best endeavour, his legs, which had gone numb, wouldn't function. He told us later that he was absolutely confident that everything would be alright from the moment he heard angels singing as they twanged their harps.

'Somehow, I was brought alongside him,' he continued. 'It was rather odd, and I'm not completely certain how it happened, but the chap looking after me turned to the chap looking after him and said "Wot's yours?" meaning what was wrong with the geezer with the beard. Doc could not stand it any more, "Mine's a double Scotch," he cried.'

Now the whole business is rather remarkable because as I mentioned earlier doctors seldom are good patients and the rescue man told me that my friend created like a wild thing when they tried to move him. He clutched at them savagely, trying to steady himself. That might have been their fault. They thought he had hurt his chest when in fact he had broken his pelvis. His neighbour had a broken spine, and got so cold he could not feel his feet, or was that cord damage?

They had a wonderful Christmas, because when they awakened, both felt warm and well. Doc's pelvis healed quite miraculously and the neighbour regained sensation in his feet; but one bottle of whisky was quite dead and a second bottle was in such low spirits that scarcely a smell remained. Only some photographs testify to the facts.

5²

Top Level First Aider
What the Casualty Expects

I believe that this small volume is perhaps the most important document Casualties Union has produced. It deals with a wide coverage — approach; examination for injury; bandaging; giving a drink; giving warmth and protection; lifting and carriage; and finally, attending to personal problems of the casualty. Each section is illuminated by comments which help to give quality to the first aider's actions. I hope everyone who reads these notes will seek out a copy and make much use of them. Suffice it here to give the Foreword and the Introduction.

FOREWORD

This publication dealing with the requirements of the 'top level first aider', together with its companion volume *The Atlas of Injury*, highlights the needs for the highest standard of training of all those who are engaged in providing any form of casualty service and wish to become proficient in first aid.

There is an ever increasing number of accidents and some people, too, seem to be accident prone, so that there is an urgent need to improve the services available for those casualties requiring immediate attention and treatment. Not only has the first aider to deal with the physical condition of the patient, and to have first rate knowledge of the treatment required for whatever injury may be sustained, but there is also the emotional state that may need help. This may be out of all proportion to the physical injury. In these cases it is the approach to the patient which is of such importance, and much can be done to lessen the effects. Sympathy, explanation, reassurance and persuasion can all be employed, but this human approach needs training and experience too. Proficiency in these arts will increase the influence of the first aider over his patient.

It is in this field that Casualties Union personnel, with their heightened sensitivity to the approach of the first aider, the handling and treatment given, can help to bring home to the learner what the effect of the treatment has been, by recollecting the impressions it made on their minds. The top level first aider will have made his training really worthwhile when he has learnt to think of what he does from the aspect of the casualty, and succeeds in treating a human personality and not just an injury.

H. L. GLYN HUGHES
President of Casualties Union

London. September, 1962

INTRODUCTION

In the twenty-first year of its existance as a specialist organization, Casualties Union has this unique contribution to make in the furtherance of first aid training — the studied point of view of the casualty.

Until the skilled casualty became an indispensable part of the training programme, by bridging the gap between knowledge and experience, it was impossible for instructors and students to estimate the effect of treatments, let alone the finer aspects of approach and handling. Now, with the greatly increased perception of trained casualty acting, new elements can be added to enliven all practical courses in first aid. It has become possible to teach approach and diagnosis, considerate examination and sensitive handling. The whole business of helping injured and distressed people has become humanized through the skill and awareness of specially trained individuals who are prepared to take their place while others practise first aid. Acting on behalf of the real casualties of the future has become a skilled art in itself.

Readers of this booklet will realize more keenly than ever the enormous importance of training the critical faculty of those who act as casualties, so that their constructive comments after being handled can greatly enhance the value of every first aid practice, competition or other event. It also becomes very obvious that the responsibility of trained casualties indulging in this type of criticism is very high.

The observations and comments in these pages have been collated from answers to a searching questionnaire completed by some fifty of the most discerning and experienced of the senior members of Casualties Union, who, collectively, have been handled by hundreds of thousands of first aiders during twenty years. Some of these have been beginners; some with more experience, and some have been truly expert; but all have left with the casualties a number of impressions. those at the receiving end feel able to say what qualities they would hope, more than that, expect to find, in being handled by the very best first aider.

These hopes and expectations have been written in readable form by members of the editorial panel of *Casualty Simulation*, the quarterly magazine in which the material first appeared. It will take its place with the companion volumes of *The Atlas of Injury* in the library of every first aid instructor and serious student of this life saving art.

Make sure YOU do not miss out by failing to read this booklet.

53

How I Became A CUCU

The Editor of *Casualty Simulation* asked several members and medical advisers how they came to be involved as fully trained casualties.

— In a stupor of stalemate from teaching first aid, I dreamt that my pupils were medical students and I a hospital doctor, all gathered round the broken legs of the shocked patient eagerly absorbing the textbook facts from life. 'What you need are trained acting casualties,' Eric whispered, 'We have them!' I was in like a shot.

General Practitioner

— It was my first Civil Defence Exercise! Casualties? I could cope with anything — I had just passed the first aid examination!! The unforgettable shock of finding 'real' casualties, with broken limbs, dreadful wounds, blood actually flowing. What lessons I learned! At Falfield while on a course, someone mentioned Casualties Union to me, and my own Study Circle was born.

Civil Defence Instructor

— I was terribly squeamish at the sight of blood or the talk of injuries, but I was very anxious to be able to help my workmates in the pit should an accident happen, without becoming a fainting casualty myself. I went along to a Casualties Union demonstration nine years ago, and realized that this was the answer. I pour the blood on myself now!

Coal Miner

— Textbook! I knew it from cover to cover. You have to when you are working your way up in a national first aid competition. And my team got to the top twice. Then we stalled. Interest flagged. What was the good of it all? 'Why not take a look at the other side,' my superior officer suggested. A new door opened and I never looked back. Now I am training lots of other teams by leading a group of Casualties Union.

First Aid Team Leader

— They'd got something, these casualties. The way they lay about on the cold, wet ground, with their raggy clothes and their realistic injuries. They brought the best out of me, and tears to my eyes. That was something a labelled body on the floor could never do. This was IT — I wanted more. So I joined with them and now I lie on the floor myself.

Industrial Nurse

— I saw the need for trained casualties so I wrote to Casualties Union H.Q. When I was advised to start my own Study Circle I was disgusted, but the C.D.O. was keen and we started it together, by collecting fourteen other martyrs with myself as the Study Circle Leader. And here I am six years later, still loving it!

Assistant Civil Defence Officer

54

Stevenage Road Safety Week — 1958
Trained Casualties Helped

Stevenage Road Safety Committee decided to lay emphasis upon the importance of pedestrian crossings. Posters were distributed throughout the town and a mobile cinema provided by the Royal Society for the Prevention of Accidents toured factories, schools and clubs throughout the week.

On the final Saturday, a live zebra paraded up and down the main street preceded by the town cryer and sandwich men and followed by more sandwich men and a jester buffooning his way through the crowd bearing the notice, 'I MAY BE A FOOL, BUT I AM SAFETY MINDED.'

The mobile cinema toured all the shopping centres announcing that demonstrations were to follow. As it drew away a police car took over giving commentaries on live 'accidents' staged by members of Casualties Union. As the commentary began a man was seen lying near the kerb with his belongings strewn all over the roadside. The police officer told the public:

'ATTENTION PLEASE. This is Hertfordshire County Police and this is Stevenage Road Safety Week. Do not be alarmed. These are not real accidents but have been staged as cautionary tales for the Stevenage Road Safety Committee by a national organization known as Casualties Union. The victim might be YOU, and the difference between a minor injury and a disaster with fatal results is so slight — perhaps only one thousandth of a second. Keep yourself safe and don't risk others. Cross at the zebra crossing.

'This man was courteous. He stepped off the kerb to avoid other pedestrians. His back was towards the traffic. He was lucky to escape with bruises and a cut over the eye. If his head, arm or leg had fallen under the car wheels, he might have been killed or maimed for life. At best he must have suffered greatly and the privations must have fallen also upon his wife, family, employers and friends.'

At this stage the agitated driver of the car was doing what he could to assist the victim and the county ambulance arrived heralded by its stirring bell. The crowd gathered closer.

The commentator continued, 'Accidents on the roads cost the country about £200 million each year. Your money. Many other people are delayed and inconvenienced. Casualties must occupy beds in hospitals that could otherwise accommodate sick persons. The effect covers the whole population. Half the road casualties are pedestrians and one-fifth are cyclists. Make room for others; don't risk their lives. Keep safe. This is Stevenage Road Safety Week. Don't permit accidents to happen. the victim could be YOU. Cross at the ZEBRA CROSSING.'

Moving a little farther down the street, it was found that a woman with a heavy shopping basket swinging on the handlebars, had fallen off her bicycle trying to avoid a pedestrian who walked straight out of a shop and across the road, without looking. The police gave a similar commentary explaining how the accident could have been avoided.

A little later a pedestrian who had been waiting uncertainly to cross the road decided to make a dash for the other side. He slipped on a banana carelessly dropped in the road and fell. His papers flew in all directions. A car stopped short and the man banged his shoulder hard against the nearside front wheel of the car, his head in front of the wheel. To bring this near miss home even more to the crowd, a woman fainted among them. The commentator again drew attention to the causes and the possible effects. He made no reference to the fainting woman. The generous public took care of her.

These accidents were repeated thirteen times during a

bitterly cold day so that as many people as possible might have the opportunity of seeing them. The road safety committee expressed the opinion that the road safety week had been a great success and that 'the splendid contribution of members of Casualties Union to the final day's activities added so much to its outstanding success.'

55

Stevenage Road Safety Display — 1960

Determined to bring their annual road safety exhibition to the notice of the public, Stevenage Road Safety Committee organized a display throughout the town on Saturday, 9th July. The junior accident prevention council co-operated and provided a little light relief as well as daintiness to the otherwise stern proceedings. They were dressed with a hat like a child's building block (most appropriate in a new town) lettered in big bright red characters so that the group spelt S-T-E-V-E-N-A-G-E from whatever direction they were seen. They carried miniature road signs on the end of wands and wore sandwich boards alternatively advertising the exhibition and 'honour your code' safety posters. They processed through the immediate area to attract attention and hand out leaflets. As they passed, a casualty was found lying in the gutter; he had stepped off the kerb with his back to the traffic and had been knocked down. The appearance of an ambulance with bell ringing followed by a police car drew the people together.

As this ended we saw that a young woman had been knocked off her bicycle by the sudden opening of a car door. The accident might have been serious. There she was, angry — bleeding nose and blood stained blouse, damaged nylons and grazed knees — but she could have been killed. TAKE CARE HOW YOU OPEN THAT DOOR.

He saw the car all right, but the stupid young fellow reckoned he could make a dash for it, not reckoning on the

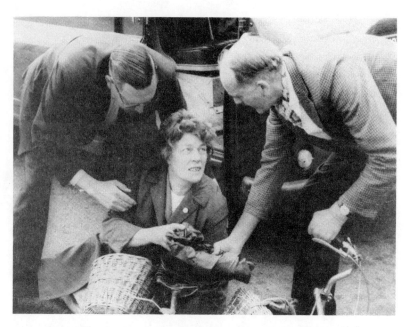

Mary Murphy is a casualty in Stevenage Road Safety Week

untidy bounder who dropped a banana skin on the road. Our young man went down with a nasty crack and the car swung high on its springs as it stopped dead. He was lucky too but he broke his collar bone and grazed his knees. KEEP THE ROADS TIDY FOR SAFETY'S SAKE. WAIT UNTIL THE ROAD IS CLEAR.

The fourth accident was caused by a man stepping out between two vehicles waiting at the kerbside. A woman passing on her cycle wobbled in trying to avoid him. Her heavy shopping basket slipped on her handlebars and she fell off. There she lay sprawled in the road for all to see surrounded by smashed eggs and scattered groceries, and to make matters worse a broken bottle of milk. Like the other victims the promoters permitted her to get off lightly, but the lessons were clear to see. STEP OUT CAUTIOUSLY FROM BEHIND VEHICLES. AVOID AWKWARD LOADS. CLEAR UP BROKEN GLASS AND SLIPPERY SUBSTANCES. The deputy town clerk stepped smartly into the road and swept it into a dustpan. A small boy with

238

an enormous load staggered across the road under the guidance of a policeman to press home the point of awkward loads.

Finally the children with their sandwich boards came back to chant the kerb drill and to cross the road. Quickly into the transport and they were off to the next place, wherever there was a parade of shops. Everyone enjoyed it. What is more everyone was talking about it.

The police took the opportunity of instructing the people upon how the accident had been caused and how it could have been avoided. WHEN WALKING WITH YOUR BACK TO THE TRAFFIC, KEEP WELL AWAY FROM THE KERB.

One police road safety officer commented in passing that the effect of the demonstrations remained effective for about three months for those who saw them.

56

Pioneering Overseas

Casualty simulation was a new art to Malaya in 1956 when members of the Royal Army Medical Corps introduced it to the first aid societies by demonstrating at competitions and courses. John Harrison of the Institute for Medical Research brought news of Casualties Union from England and together they formed the first Study Circle in Kuala Lumpur, Selangor, under the leadership of Staff-Sergeant Ivor York.

Early efforts were devoted to propaganda and demonstrations. After a private show in the C.D. Corps' ruined house, police permission was obtained to show the results of a car crash outside the Secretariat in Kuala Lumpur. Radio Malaya provided the sound effects leading up to the crash, and a doctor who thought that a real accident had occurred offered his help right away.

The first proficiency test was observed by Lt.-Col. Jackson-Smythe, Capt. P. H. Setna and doctor J. J. Cronin of the R.A.M.C., and eleven candidates passed up to full membership. Now a second Study Circle has started with the only remaining European, John Kemmett of the R.A.F., as its secretary. It is a truly international body, comprising Malays, Indians and Chinese, following such diverse religions as Islam, Hinduism, Buddhism, Sikhism, Confucianism and Christianity. You will hear more of this circle under the leadership of Miss Lim Leng Chee.

☆　　☆　　☆

Miss Pauline Wallis, a teacher from New Zealand, has been in the United Kingdom for two years and has now returned to her own country, where her father is an officer of St. John and a keen reader of Casualty Simulation. Towards the end of her stay in England, Mr. Wallis wrote to Pauline suggesting that she visit Casualties Union. This proved a most happy event; Pauline joined London branch as a probationer and passed her proficiency test on 28th January, 1959. Pauline received her membership from the hand of Eric Claxton a fortnight later. Pauline has endeared herself to all members of London Branch and they join with the officers and other members of the union in wishing her a happy homecoming in New Zealand and a speedy return to England. We all hope that her skill as a trained casualty will be of assistance to her fellow countrymen and that Pauline will be only the first of many members in her district. Miss Pauline Wallis lives in Christchurch, c/o H. S. Wallis, Esq., St. John Ambulance Brigade, 55/61 Peterborough Street, Christchurch, C.1., New Zealand.

☆　　☆　　☆

Mrs. E. M. Callard has established S.C.388 in Windhoek, S.W.A. She writes on 22nd October, 1959, 'We have at the moment seven members. Dr. Jacobson has agreed to attend as often as he can, and as he usually goes to the hospital first in the evenings, it suits us very well if he turns up about 9 p.m. We have to date done the faking of simple wounds on the hand, face and elbow, and then describing how the injury happened, and then each one goes out, comes in again and acts the injury. We spent nearly the whole of two evenings learning how to faint, and more important, how to fall, and it is becoming much easier. The actual coming out of the faint was real fun, for the doctor sat in an easy chair, and pulled each one to bits and then built one up again. It is rather fantastic how one can think oneself into a situation, and then act it out. It is sometimes difficult, for then we get the giggles, but the threat of a one shilling fine for the kitty to buy material has considerably

241

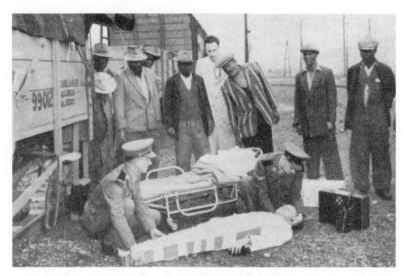

Practice in South Africa

reduced that hazard. Personally I am getting a lot of fun out of it, for all the hard work, and we have all agreed that this is not the training to give someone with hypochondriac tendencies.

It has not rained here for about six months, and it is stinking hot. The application of make-up to the face to show shock just drips off!! It is hardly necessary in any case, for most of us look pale and drawn, with black rings under our eyes, so much can be done with altering the expression in the face and eyes. We work in old clothes, khaki for the men, and slacks and blouses for the women, with bare feet, and so it is bearable.

Le Maquillage des Accidents. By Emelie Berry — Edinburgh Red Cross and Waverley Branch C.U.

I had the honour of being picked by the British Red Cross Society to lead the delegation from Great Britain for the First International Study Centre for First Aid, held at Versailles in mid-July, 1960. This was because I had French as my native language and had made a study of casualty simulation.

Nine countries were invited and eight were able to send representatives. Belgium had so much trouble abroad at the time and were unable to come. Teams came from France, Germany, Switzerland, Luxembourg, Spain, Italy, The Netherlands and Great Britain.

Four subjects were being studied: stretcher bearing, fractures, haemorrhage and asphyxiation. Three quarters of the time was given to practical work. Each subject was introduced by a team and each team in turn demonstrated their particular methods of treatment. The aim was to determine the methods which European countries had in common and where we differed, and eventually to standardise first aid methods.

A whole day was devoted to casualty simulation — *le maquillage des accidents*. This was led by Great Britain. I began my talk by listing our materials for make-up. I then demonstrated a bruise, a simple wound, a simple fracture, an open fracture of tibia and fibula, and made up a patient for shock. We were followed by Switzerland who demonstrated burns, and Luxembourg who prefabricated their wounds with a rubbery material on which the injury was painted. It looked very clumsy. France used a whole set of prefabricated wounds which were amazingly realistic. The whole outfit was in a white metal box and was made in Norway. The complete set cost about £20.

The majority of the countries were most interested in the British method of casualty simulation, and particular interest was shown when I went on to stress the tremendous importance of staging and acting, especially the acting and reacting to bad and good handling, thus emphasising the fact that the person acting must know the correct and wrong treatment of injuries.

57

Stretcher Carrying and Ambulance Loading
by a Casualty

Just how much can one be jolted upon a stretcher? An involuntary shudder passes through one as one contemplates the question. I am only a 'casualty' and I am constantly surprised. Nobody seems to bother about this part of training. It usually feels to me as if one bearer has a wooden leg, while another is twelve inches shorter than his partner, and each of them changes hands each step! I realize that I may be wronging a number of instructors by that comment, but I suppose I haven't been carried on a stretcher by their 'bods'.

When I heard that the Civil Defence Competition on C.U. Day was to be devoted to stretcher carrying, I was delighted. This will show 'em, I said. But do you know what those stupid organizers did — well, they overdid it, I reckon. They went to elaborate trouble to prepare a stretcher with a special table on it to carry a fearsome array of gadgets for recording the vibrations. They balanced it carefully with bags of earth secured under the platform so that it weighed and balanced as though a ten stone man was lying on it.

They also included things called 'tell-tales', if you please — I could tell better tales than these. But what really happened was this — now I'm telling you — the bearers took fright lest one of these machines fell off and got busted, so they were frightfully careful.

These tell-tales I was speaking about consisted of nine-pins (actually there were ten) with fairy bells tied on them so that, when they fell, they tinkled prettily. There was also a dish of blood, or ink, or some red liquid that spilled onto a sheet of white blotting paper. The bearers, as well as the spectators, could see it spill. They could hear the pins fall too, so they were extra-super-duper-frightfully careful. It was these stupid tell-tales 'cos they wouldn't have been like that at all if I had been on the stretcher — but then I weigh eleven stone three.

It gives you an idea when I tell you it took them five or six minutes to carry the stretcher about twenty yards and place it on the lower berth of an ambulance. The tests were — raise, turn and carry, set down; raise, climb kerb, and set down; raise, descend kerb, set down; load ambulance, bottom right berth.

The four stages were timed separately, because the rules set a limit of ten minutes, as if anyone could take ten minutes over that. Even so some of the teams couldn't keep the nine-pins standing, though the winners, Chorley 'A' from the Royal Ordnance Factory, did not lose the tenth until the fourth test. They also managed to avoid spilling any appreciable 'blood' until the fourth test.

The kerbs caused trouble to all teams and so did the ambulance loading. I reckon that teams who kept the pins standing longest were bound to do best, but you can't have nine-pins on a stretcher. Perhaps next year we could have the machines hidden, so the bearers could not see what was happening. We've got to make it so they learn to carry a stretcher properly at a proper speed without jolting and without tell-tales.

It will need a lot of practice, but it can be done. At any rate it will provide some of the most exciting training, judging by the interest shown by the teams. Good luck too, I say, and thank you for being careful.

☆　　☆　　☆

The *Official Report* for 1960 drew conclusions as follows:

The contest showed the need for much practice in

stretcher carrying and even more important in ambulance loading. It demonstrated the need for developing a technique of good carrying at a reasonable pace by a well-balanced team under good leadership. From this there is need to develop the technique so that any bearer can drop into any team without material loss of cushioned carriage.

There may be nothing wrong with the accredited drills of stretcher bearing, but training and practice appear to need greater attention.

The discipline necessary for this higher standard of stretcher bearing — the team work — the harmony — the gentleness developed out of skill and strength — must have one of the most valuable effects upon the development of the ambulanceman's skill as a first aider or rescuer.

It is recommended that further competitions should be staged. A much briefer time schedule should be introduced to increase the speed. A period of ninety seconds should be adequate for a similar contest. It is recommended that tell-tales or indicators should be kept invisible to the bearers to avoid destroying the rhythm.

The committee acknowledged the assistance given by the Railway Executive, the Ministry of Aviation, Civil Defence as well as to the judges, timekeepers, marshalls and the teams.

In later years only the pannikin of 'blood' and the blotting paper target has been retained as a tell-tale and the whole area of the target is covered so the bearers are unable to see whether or not they have caused any spillage. Gradually the competitors needed more challenge than up and down kerbs and loading into an ambulance. They sought more adventurous routes over which they must carry the stretcher, which has always been loaded as for a ten stone person and of course heavier at one end. The contest continues to be judged by lowest time plus minimum spillage of 'blood' together, the minimal distance thrown, as revealed by the 'blood' pattern on the blotting paper target.

58

We Would Like You To Meet
Some More of The Stalwarts

AILEEN POULTON. For infectious vitality and dynamic personality you could call at St. Mark's Vicarage, Exeter, and meet the vicar's wife. She might be planning some Casualties Union exploit, but that would only be in the intervals between helping her husband with the work of his large parish, running a Red Cross detachment or working part-time on the nursing staff of the Exeter City Hospital. But whatever she was doing, Aileen Poulton would have time to talk to you about the excitement of acting as a casualty or the horrors of organizing a first aid competition.

Headlines in the local press — 'Vicar's wife found hanging in the orchard!' It would only be Mrs. Poulton up to her tricks again at an exercise for the Exeter police team.

When she enrolled in Casualties Union in 1950, she modestly described herself as housewife — a gross understatement. To her husband and four children she is a beloved partner and help-mate; to her hosts of friends a tower of strength, and to the flourishing Exeter branch of C.U. its enthusiastic organizer who has led it through many difficulties since it was a struggling Study Circle. Those who have worked with Aileen Poulton on any project agree that it is a privilege to know her.

WILLIAM BROMFIELD. 'It all depends on the tides,' is the usual answer one gets when asking Bill Bromfield to undertake a job for C.U. or St. John Ambulance Brigade. For the tide is about the only thing that will stop him working all day for first aid. We believe that in his *spare* time he is a berthing master on the Humber River at Hull, Kingston. Early in 1950 he realized the advantages of having trained casualties and formed a group of Casualties Union in Hull through which he gained his instructorship. He was made a serving brother of the Order of St. John in 1952 and now he combines his work for both organizations. Keenly interested in competitions he swopped over from the competing side to the promotion of first aid training through competitions and among others now organises the George Richardson Competition each year in Hull.

A glutton for work, his colleagues say he does too much, but Bill can't see that at all. He combines dogged determination with even-tempered judgement. His marvellous patience and sincerity are what endear him to his friends and make him so dependable in his work and his hobbies.

☆ ☆ ☆

H. F. SKIDMORE. There are some characters who become legendary in their own lifetime, and one of these was 'Skiddy'. He was present at an instructor course held in Reading in January 1946 and very soon after became the organizer of the Reading branch. About a year later he was appointed librarian of C.U. (Yes! In those days we had a postal library of technical books bearing on our subjects.) In 1948 he gained his instructorship.

Skiddy was an individualist, not always easy to get on with, but his kindness and generosity were unforgettable. There can hardly be a member who knew him who had not been the recipient of sweets and fruit he liberally dispensed on C.U. Day to hard pressed casualties. His sense of precision and intense responsibility were part of his professional attitude of mind, for Skiddy was a crack express engine driver hauling the famous trains which plied between Paddington and Bristol. On his reliability depended

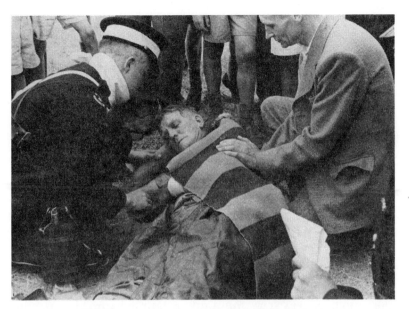
Skiddy as a casualty at Pressed Steel, Oxford

the comfort and safety of many thousands of passengers. I wonder how many paused to thank him as the giant loco rested at the end of each journey?

We say 'Thank You' to him now at the end of *his* journey, as did the representatives of six organizations in which he was interested when his coffin, draped with the St. J.A.B. flag bearing his cap and medals, paused for two minutes outside the Reading St. John Ambulance Hall, of which he was founder and trustee, as a mark of respect. We share the loss with his widow, Mrs. Grace Skidmore, who tells us how bravely he bore the last ten months of suffering. As a dedicated member of C.U. he would understand suffering.

MRS. F. E. BARRETT. 'Floss' Barrett, leader of Altrincham Branch since it began died on 29th January, 1969. She gave a lifetime of service to B.R.C.S., entwined inseparably since 1951 with C.U. ideas and ideals. In particular she found trained patients invaluable in teaching home nursing, even using them to show the need for special diets.

The vast host of those who bade adieu to her on a crisp winter's day, bore testimony to Floss's boundless interests and to her gift for friendship. It is a mark of her courage that she concealed her fears and suffering, believing that it was her duty and privilege to spread happiness and the warm hospitality of her lovely cottage and garden as long as God would give her strength.

We who loved her cannot, therefore, be sad that her pain is over, but rejoice that she passed our way and enriched us with her genteel and gracious charm.

☆　　☆　　☆

TED ALDRIDGE. It was always difficult to believe that Ted was only acting and not really ill or hurt. He had the most amazing capacity for thinking himself into the part he was playing, and if ever there was a member of C.U. who could be said to be a 'natural', it was Ted. He could twist one's heartstrings with the pathetic way in which he appealed to the tenderest emotions of which one was capable.

In the *Nursing Mirror* competition for teams from the National Association of State Enrolled Nurses' training schools, Ted was a bed-ridden patient having been 'operated on' the previous day for chole cystectomy. The nurses made him comfortable as best they could, but he had to give place to Pip Gilardi a road accident casualty brought in five minutes later. All who saw his performance were convinced that he was in urgent need of the most skilled nursing.

He was greatly involved in the pioneer work done at Netherne Hospital where C.U. trained mental patients act in groups for the assessment of inter-personal relationships between student nurses and their charges. Apart from his convincing performances in this capacity, which could move one to tears, he was almost overwhelmingly grateful to C.U. for having taught him the art of casualty acting, whereas we would all say we learned an enormous amount from watching him.

In his retirement, Ted continued his work with B.R.C.S. as an escort, and for the Children's Country Holiday Fund he would travel up and down the country shepherding parties of children on their way to and from holiday homes. By his death we lost one of our 'elder statesmen'.

SIDNEY FRANCIS. Sidney was one of the founder members of Casualties Union who gave tremendous service to Civil Defence and First Aid in the war years and in the re-formative years after the war. He was a warden in the Woking C.D. when we first knew him as a frequent 'casualty' at the Rescue School at Leatherhead. Professionally Sidney was a photographer with a studio in Woking, and he gave unstintingly of his skill and resources to the union. He was responsible for all the photographs in the original brochure which was published by the union just after the end of the war in 1945. A splendid tribute from him to C.U. He was an artist with a camera. He had a wonderful sense of the exact moment to click the shutter, and how to capture the truest expression in his life-like portraiture.

It was, however, Sidney the man whom we all loved. His face would crinkle up into a radiant smile and he would volunteer long before you could ask him to do you a service. He gave his services, whether just personal or professional, for Sidney was a great giver.

We who knew him well will miss him greatly, but one thing is certain, we shall never forget him. He had that delightful sort of unforgettable personality.

FRANK SHORT. If ever you want to find a man truly dedicated to the welfare of his fellow men, to whom distance and trouble taken are the negligible cost of service, and in whom devotion to duty is wrapped up in a delightfully kind and happy personality, you need never look further than Haven Lane, Oldham in Lancashire.

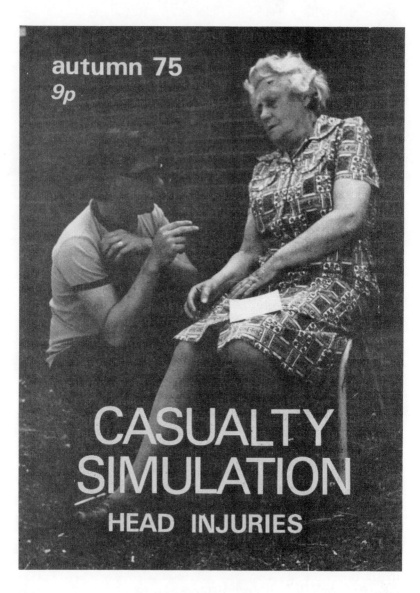

autumn 75
9p

CASUALTY
SIMULATION
HEAD INJURIES

Doris Harris on the cover of
Casualty Simulation

We have had the privilege of knowing Frank since 1957 when he found the answer to his first aid teaching by joining the Altrincham branch of C.U. to train as a casualty. He soon proved himself to be a first class casualty and his administrative ability made the steps to instructorship easy going. He was a natural choice for senior instructorship, for his knowledge of C.U. and enthusiasm for its aims and methods are outstanding. A man capable of giving shrewd judgments and most acceptably constructive criticism, both of himself and others, he is of incalculable value in an organization like ours.

A family man himself, he and his wife, Marjorie, have always been devoted to young people. Frank has a tremendous record of help to Scouts, Guides, Boy's Brigade, Police Cadets and school children working for the Duke of Edinburgh's Award, in giving them all realistic training in first aid. Red Cross first aid and nursing teams prepared by Frank for their annual competitions have reached their national finals on several occasions. And of course, as B.R.C.S. training officer for the East Lancashire branch, Frank says he simply could not teach first aid without the use of skilled casualties at every stage. The British Red Cross honoured him in the 60s with the award of their Certificate of Honour and Badge, Class III, for over thirty years work through the society. We know that he gave a great deal of time to Civil Defence too. The Catholic Handicapped Children's Fellowship claims him once a month at least, when he helps with the work of making it more possible for mentally and physically crippled children to take as active a part in life as they can. Entertainment and transport are only a small part of what he does for them.

In his spare time Frank earns his living as a warehouse manager in Manchester! We never know how he manages to fit this into his very full weeks. Altrincham is a shade further away still from Oldham, but Frank attends the activities of the C.U. branch there as though it was just round the corner. Teamwork begins at home, and Marjorie, his wife, is a helper member of Casualties Union. It is undoubtedly a privilege to have Frank and Marjorie sharing their first love with C.U.

☆   ☆   ☆

MISS K. W. M. (KAY) BOWRING. Kay died on 10th February, 1984 in her late seventies after a year of failing health. Kay was a mathematician and a close colleague of Miss M. E. (Phil) Philbrick a historian, both of whom were teachers at a secondary school in Truro. These activities failed to satisfy either of them and they thought to try horticulture. Before they gave up their teaching jobs they set out to grow violets as a venture on the side in the garden of their cottage well away from the city.

Both these ladies possessed tremendous energy and drive and their zeal for public service was an inspiration to many, growing rather than diminishing during the war and after until at the end of Kay's life she was still involved in many projects of general interest.

Urged perhaps by necessity for food production during the war, having given up teaching, they moved to 'Algarnick', Carnon Down, outside Truro, where they grew vegetables and also looked after two farms in the vicinity. A busy life one might say, but both were air raid wardens and belonged also to the Red Cross.

Kay was a Red Cross instructor in life saving before being party to the formation of Casualties Union Study Circle 88, Truro, in February, 1951 and passed into full membership in August of the same year — the founder is reputed to have been tough with this study circle, which obviously had a great potential, because they staged outdoor scenes in Red Cross H.Q. A year later Kay became an instructor for C.U. and in due season a senior instructor. Her natural flair for teaching was an asset to both C.U. and Red Cross. In peacetime Kay concentrated on growing daffodils and strawberries in partnership with Phil.

Hospitable to a fault, she had the wisdom to teach her willing guests how to pick, pack and dispatch the garden produce in time for next day's London market. I felt privileged to be permitted to share in these activities and would never go to Cornwall without visiting her home.

Nancy Budgett recalls 'meeting this strong character for the first time at the C.U. Reunion held at Hay's Wharf, London Bridge in October, 1950, where Kay demanded to know everything and insisted on seeing Eric Claxton.'

In retirement from Red Cross, C.U. and market gardening at the same time, Kay devoted her life to researching the human side of life in Old Cornwall; how people lived, dressed, cooked, and earned their meagre living, local crafts, why some migrated, local superstitions, religions, dances and fertility rites. She took up painting with mathematical care for perspective — Kay's buildings always stood up and were most attractive.

Her native humour, cheerfulness and charm never deserted her. She had many friends, all of whom mourn her loss but most of all her constant companion Phil, to whom we extend our sincerest sympathy. Kay's life was well lived and we may best sum up our feelings by thanking God for Kay's life and for permitting us in some small way to share it.

NANCY M. BUDGETT

☆　　☆　　☆

NORMAN WRIDE. An enthusiastic instructor Norman was always willing to be called upon to cope with the days problems however difficult they might be.

Norman Wride

Archie Elliot

ARCHIE ELLIOTT. Archie died on 12th February, 1968. We in Newcastle-Upon-Tyne branch will miss him greatly. It was a privilege to have shared his friendship. He was one of those rare characters, finely chiselled from the qualities of greatness. For over forty of his seventy years he worked far down below the sea off the Northumberland coast as a coal miner, often up to his knees in water. He laughingly told us that the reason he did not suffer from rheumatism was because it was sea-water! Many were the stories of his days down the pit, and he reckoned he owed his life to his pit pony who once stopped dead in his tracks and would not budge forward. Seconds later the roof came down and blocked the way ahead with tons of stone. Bobby's sharp ears had heard the ominous cracking sound of imminent disaster.

In his retirement Archie took up gardening and found that he had green fingers, and his membership of Red Cross led him to become a trained casualty, and we found he was a 'natural'. No time was too early to start from home and no discomfort too great to 'suffer' in the cause. His dry sense of humour and his ability to laugh at himself endeared him to all who knew him. His utter sincerity and reliability was a great strength to us. His hands were hard with toil as his nature was gentle and patient, with an intimate knowledge of how much we depend upon appreciation of the things of the earth for our glimpses of heaven. We can hear him now 'My heavens, yes,' or 'My heavens, no,' when we asked his views on things, and if anybody knew that, 'Heaven lies about us', it was Archie Elliott.

WILLIAM C. WARNE. Founder members will be sad to learn of the death of Bill, who was such a splendid and indefatigable casualty actor during the days at Leatherhead. When one passed his garage business at Shalford crossroads, we are all reminded of those pioneering days. A splendid, reliable and generous worker in the cause of realism in Civil Defence. Bill will be long remembered. Our thanks and condolences go out to his family.

59

Instructorship

Instructorship is an institution so *others* may learn. It
demands the presentation of each subject so that others may
understand and become able to deal with situations and
problems within the faculty they wish to learn.

It demands, therefore, the ability to identify with each
student, which in turn demands the *total giving of oneself*. For
many people this is the hardest part of being an instructor;
yet it is fundamental to overcoming shyness, embarrassment,
nervousness and failure to find the right words and actions,
and it enables the creation of an absolute rapport with each
student.

Giving oneself may seem an enormous demand upon your
personality, but it is the basis of all meaningful relationships
so it is not too great to grant to a friend.

The instructor's *aim* has many facets which develop as
progress is made. Let us look at some of them.

A — attract
I — interest
M — memorable

So immediately we see the importantance of giving
oneself in this context. The aim quickly unfolds to

A — alert
I — inform
M — motivate

And the emphasis has moved over from you to them. As they approach each situation they will learn

A — assess
I — invent
M — manipulate

As the rapport develops the A — I — M will present other facets.

Good instructors keep every topic simple; you can learn everything about make-up from a discrete one inch cut that bleeds. One can know how good is the result by the simple yardstick of realism, which is the *only* standard. When realism has been achieved with a small cut, or blister, or bruises, there is no problem in greater grosser injuries for the techniques are truly the same and the standard should *never* be less. Loss of realism comes as much from the failure to match cause and effect as from any other reason; each injury, or, indeed, illness is different though it may exhibit similarities. Think, therefore, very carefully what caused the one inch cut and how, so that its location and shape may be apposite.

If anything conflicts with realism, even the ordinary man in the street would spot it and realize that the whole thing was phoney. I recall one day at Leatherhead when a party of forty M.O.H. who were on an administrative course at C.D. Staff College at Stoke d'Abernon, were sent to visit the rescue school so we could teach them how to teach first aid in wartime. I pictured myself teaching my 'grandmother to suck eggs' and determined to have two 'accidents' during their visit.

They arrived by coach and I chose the place for them to alight where I was waiting to greet them. I began to escort them across the site to the wooden hut which served as a lecture room. As soon as they were all in sight of the most damaged part of the building — an instructor high up in the wreckage yelled our 'look out below', and came rushing down to the ground to attend to the situation — out of the clouds of fine dust (finely sieved ashes) staggered a woman, Brenda Whiteley, with a discrete cut on her forehead which was bleeding profusely bloodying her blouse and she was

Incident at Rescue School, Leatherhead

plastered with dust and debris. She was obviously badly shaken but was most concerned as she ran up to me, that she had inadvertantly ruined the afternoon's programme. I played up appropriately, displeased but keeping my cool, telling her not to worry but to go and have a rest and get cleaned up. Then I had a brainwave — all those doctors — readily two of them volunteered to take care of her, while the rest of them commiserated with me for having such a mishap during their visit.

Some ten minutes later the two doctors rejoined the company saying that it had taken them all that time to realize that it was *not* an accident they had witnessed — just our method of routine training. After that it became possible for us to instruct them in how to teach first aid in wartime.

Later, however, we met our Waterloo. A rescue man was working on a tunnel through a five hundred ton pile of debris, when suddenly all went quiet. He had stopped working when suddenly there was a strong smell of town gas. In those days town gas was lethal and a pungent smell was added to all supplies as a warning. The alarm was given and another rescue man wearing remote breathing apparatus worked his way down the tunnel — gradually the tunneller was brought out, he was limp, his face was pale, but he had bright red blotches on his cheeks and was not breathing.

The doctors were impressed by the rescue but totally unconcerned about the plight of the rescued tunneller, whose behaviour was most realistic — but we learnt afterwards his fingernails and wrists looked much too healthy — no need to look twice. *Total* realism is the *only* standard.

There is a terrible danger of stereotyping injuries. If an instructor shows a particular injury made up, there will be hundreds like it in a very short time. Then first aiders might come to expect all such injuries to be like that. To avoid this tendency always show the precise cause (agent and movement or action) and model accordingly. Cuts, for example can be caused in innumerable ways from a blade of grass or sheet of paper, through all the knives and chisels to tin can lids or shards of glass.

In approaching the planning, staging and mounting of an accident situation, we need once more to be aware of our aim: appreciate the problem; imagine the situation; meditate upon the human behaviour of those involved; are they strangers? Are they hurt? Have they worries? Do they panic?

All these details must be worked out.

You may find it surprising that over all these years I have never asked anybody to join Casualties Union. It is so important that we attract them to share in our activities. Membership must never be cheapened because truthfully it is very wonderful to be a member of C.U.

In an organization where there is no rank and everyone is equal, it requires real humility to be an instructor; while a senior instructor needs to maintain simplicity and sincerity and to be a peer to each and everyone of his fellow-members.

We need therefore to prepare ourselves for this special task. One way is to put your subconscious mind to work

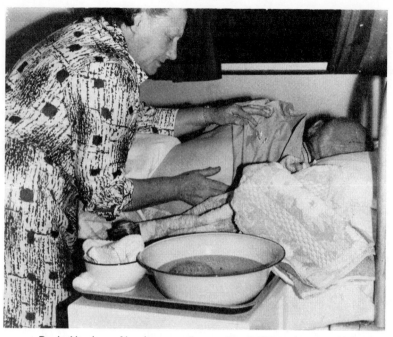

Doris Harris — Nursing practice and experience is essential

and it will do miracles for you. It is simple. Just sit down with a pencil and paper and think round the problem of being an instructor — of being *good* as an instructor and yet to remain on an equal footing with every other member, including of course, those whom you will be called upon to instruct. *They* learn and the instructor provides the *opportunities* for them. Think very hard about them, yourself and C.U. techniques. Maybe your thinking all works out nicely, but perhaps you are left with a quandary. Sleep on it for a couple of nights and surprisingly you will know very clearly the answers to the questions you have been asking yourself. The subconscious is a great ally, but remember *no* deep concentration and *no* hard thinking and there will be no response. The subconscious wants wooing. If you think hard enough you will meet others who are thinking about the same things.

A second and more powerful way of building yourself up, which you can use in association with the sub-conscious, is worth exploring. (You may be interested to know I used both these methods to build up my capacity to cope not only with C.U. but also my job in building the U.K.'s first new town, at Stevenage, for I felt woefully inadequate for such immense responsibilities.)

Sit upright in a straight-backed chair — alert but utterly relaxed. Posture is important — feet flat on the floor and hands on your knees with fingers relaxed, not clenched or clasped; eyes fixed on a single point on the other side of the room — not the clock, because then your mind will pay attention only to the passage of time. Sit quietly and still — don't move a muscle. Make your mind quite blank and try to keep it so for as long as you can. Try every day and you will be able to achieve ten minutes, fifteen, twenty, thirty, even an hour without strain and gradually the universal mind will fill yours with ideas and ability, wit and power to achieve them.

One method with concentrated thought alerts your sub-conscious. The other empties your mind of all extraneous matter and opens it to the power source of all that is good.

I have been conscious of this for a long time. In my wartime book on the use of Casualties Union technique, written shortly after C.U. was founded, which I dedicated to some of those who had inspired me — to Brenda Whiteley, Edward Akester, William Warne, James L. Barford, to other members of Casualties Union and to all who had pioneered in providing real training for Civil Defence, I added this prayer:

'Teach us, O God, to give and not to count the cost,
To fight and not to heed the wounds,
To toil and not to seek for rest,
To labour and not to seek for any reward save
    knowing that we do Thy Will.'

I believed *then* that we were called on to give ourselves and I am even more sure of this more than forty years on.

Instructorship enhances the opportunity for learning for everyone, but as an extra bonus to the instructor who has learnt to give himself — a bonus well within the reach of our membership.

60

Major Disaster Exercises

There was no lack of response when I asked for twenty volunteers to act as casualties for a combined exercise to take place at sea and on Newhaven beaches. The organizations taking part were R.N.V.R., St.J.A.B., B.R.C.S. and C.D.

It was a warm, sunny day and everyone was in high spirits as we climbed aboard *H.M.S. Isis* lying in Newhaven docks. Being an ex-Petty Officer myself I had no difficulty in understanding a seaman's instruction, 'Takum dahn aft Sir' — there wasn't very much room 'down aft' and everyone was trying to do their make-up looking and feeling like sardines. It wasn't until we got well out to sea that someone again mentioned sardines and people began to feel seasick, there was quite a heavy swell running.

In due course we arrived off Newhaven beaches, some three hundred spectators were waiting there and St. John, Red Cross and Civil Defence uniforms were prominent hustling around carrying out the orders of their officers.

Suddenly there was a big bang and a rocket came snaking towards us carrying a line — but it fell a few feet short — a second attempt however, dropped a line right across our bows, from this line a rope was pulled aboard and passed through blocks and tackle and very soon some of our casualties were having an aerial trip to shore by Breeches Buoy. The more seriously injured cases were taken in small boats. Once they were ashore they were quickly given first aid and sent to 'hospital'.

Remarks were passed about how ill the casualties looked — how much credit for this went to greasepaint and how much to seasickness I'll never know. Tough first aid men waded out to meet the incoming boats which were being thrown violently about by the swell and the landing of casualties was quite tricky. Two lady members while being lifted out had their middles dipped in the 'cruel sea' and they had to remain in this uncomfortable state until they reached home, as their change of clothing did not include etceteras. Nobody grumbled, however, and all the casualties thoroughly enjoyed the day.

The first aid was very good and I felt that many lessons were learned by First aiders, R.N.V.R. and Casualties Union alike.

H. C. EXCELL

☆   ☆   ☆

N.H.S.R. Exercise 'Gory'

Exercise 'Gory' was worked out over an area of countryside near Bicester, Oxon, on Saturday, 28th May, 1960. The situation was grim. Bicester and the surrounding area was badly knocked about but Garrison Theatre at Gravenhill Camp was intact and the senior medical officer decided to set up a Forward Medical Aid Unit in the theatre itself. This appeared to be a sound decision. There was ample space with suitable doors admitting walking cases and stretcher cases separately and others for evacuation. A rest centre was improvised nearby in a marquee.

Casualties were collected to ambulance loading points Ludgershall and Piddington. Thence they were transported by ambulance to the F.M.A.U. at Gravenhill. Walking wounded from Bicester area arrived in a desultory stream. This increased to a considerable flow as word got round that medical attention was available at Gravenhill.

Casualties Union provided nearly three hundred trained personnel and, supported by cadets who played the part of lightly wounded and homeless, they produced under the general direction of Dr Porter some thousand casualties which were fed into the F.M.A.U. in the course of the exercise. Many casualties did two and three turns to achieve this loading.

Peter Pendry from Slough branch was in charge of the casualty 'factory' at Piddington, John Wise at Ludgershall and Eric Claxton at Gravenhill. Each of them was supported by a strong team of instructor members.

It was only proper, under such pressure, that a great many of the slightly wounded were discharged without treatment, but were given rest, refreshment and suitable attention at the rest centre.

Major casualties were dressed, immobilized in plaster splints, but left in a condition in which they could help themselves as much as possible. A number of surgical operations were undertaken. Rescuscitation and sedatives were given to large numbers of the more severely injured. Kindliness was everywhere.

It had been hoped to take full advantage of the acting of the more severely injured casualties from the time of preliminary dressing before transport to the F.M.A.U. and during transport to give realistic experience to the casualty collecting services and ambulance services. In the upshot, the preliminary dressing had to be mass produced by the limited number of workers and experience of 'caring for an injured person' had to go by default. The ambulance crews were able, nevertheless, to profit by the accurate behaviour of the simulated casualties.

One is lost in admiration every time Oxford Regional Hospital Board prepares an exercise and this was no exception. The careful preparation by Colonel Ledger, Mrs. Welbrock-Smith, Dr. Porter and others ensured that lasting value accrued from the operations. The other organizations involved catch the enthusiasm and are themselves rewarded by a sense of achievement as well as experience gained.

Mrs. Welbrock-Smith in saying that the board was 'most grateful . . . for such magnificent assistance . . . to be able to save lives, and the work we (F.M.A.U.) do is purely of a life-saving nature', ended with these heartening words, 'Without your (Casualties Union) help it would be even more difficult to train these teams (F.M.A.U.).

Exercise 'Nordic'

The Salford Hospital Accident Services held an exercise on Sunday, 24th July, at Salford Docks, by permission of the Ship Canal Company. Members of Altrincham and Manchester Branches of Casualties Union had to fit in as casualties to the story. The S/S ... of 4,000 tons, was berthed at No. 9 Dock, laden with a mixed cargo including powdered caustic chemicals for unloading. A sling carrying kegs of chemicals broke from the crane hook. Two of the kegs fell to the deck of the ship and burst open, the remainder crashed on the dockside. There was an explosion which resulted in cases and bales stacked in a shed collapsing and goods on the dockside and in the shed being set ablaze. Twenty casualties were to be found strewn around and about the scene with injuries including severe burns, crush injuries, fractures of femur, pelvis, skull, jaw, an amputated arm and a penetrating abdominal wound. Some of the casualties were women and they had not to mind lying under rather alarming machinery.

All the public services took part with the doctors, sisters and nursing staff from Salford hospitals. the fire brigade got there first and did the initial first aid. The exercise was directed by Colonel Duncan D. Cranna, T.D., R.A.M.C., Consultant Orthopaedic Surgeon at Salford Royal and Commanding Officer of 12th Manchester C.C.S., R.A.M.C., some of whose men took part as slightly injured casualties. The R.S.M. spoke to a man sitting down on a seat and holding his head, 'What's up, chum?'

'God! I saw that bloody woman with the arm blown off and I thought she was real and fainted and hit my head.'

☆   ☆   ☆

Leicester County Police

Disaster training is being taken up all over the country. The county of Leicester called out its public services on Sunday 26th June to deal with a staged railway accident at

Bus and train in collision at Brighton

Glenfield Station, where three coaches of the Leicester to Coalville train had collided with a ganger's brake. The ten gangers and passengers in the train were portrayed as injured by the Leicester Study Circle of Casualties Union and others who were made-up and briefed by them. A high degree of realism was set and the exercise gained a lot of useful publicity. A surgical team from Leicester Royal Infirmary made on-the-spot diagnoses and gave 'injections' to the critically hurt passengers and gangers. An official said that it had given the public and voluntary services a first class opportunity of working as a team in the realistic conditions of a rail smash.

☆   ☆   ☆

Exercise Tunnel

This time we take you to the scene of exercise tunnel, a major disaster exercise staged at Kemp Town Station, Brighton. The bus was supposed to have been running on the road over the tunnel, left the road, careered down the embankment, but did not overturn because as it bounced over the rails it swung round and was held upright by the train. The sudden stopping of the train and the impact of the bus accounted for nearly one hundred and fifty casualties. All the town services and voluntary societies turned out to salvage the wounded.

We congratulate the British Red Cross Society of Sussex for organizing the exercise and for obtaining the co-operation of so many other authorities. We believe that the great value of the exercise lay in all the casualties being trained, which meant that everyone concerned took it all seriously. With so many major railway and air accidents in recent history, surely we cannot do less than organize and train ourselves in the mild light of day for what may happen in the fearful hours of fog and darkness. (Editorial comment in 'Casualty Simulation' to splendid photographs given to C.U. by *The Brighton Herald Limited.*)

Exercise tunnel was organized at Brighton on Sunday, 28th September, by the Sussex Branch of the British Red Cross Society, with members from London, Brighton, Eastbourne and Southampton branches of Casualties Union.

British Railways helped by loaning the site and an engine and four coaches (due to be broken up) and the Southdown Bus Co. produced a bus with the top ripped off. Brighton Police, Ambulance and Fire Services, Civil Defence, W.V.S. and four teams of St. John Ambulance Brigade took part as well as over 250 B.R.C.S. members.

Royal Sussex County Hospital provided a surgical aid team and received all the evacuated casualties, as well as lending their board room for the conference after the exercise. The headmaster of Brighton College kindly lent their gymnasium as a make-up room for casualties, which was about the only comfortable time they had.

The co-operation between the professional and voluntary services taking part in this exercise was beyond belief. The question of the day was, 'How can we help?' Sir Ivor Julian, C.B.E., commenting on the exercise said that the performance of the members of Casualties Union was really remarkable. We want them to realize how grateful we are to them for the wonderful help given by them throughout the year in routine training, competitions and major exercises.

JOHN BOSVILLE
County Director, Sussex, B.R.C.S.

From its usually sleepy, unused state, Kemp Town Station sprang into life at 9 o'clock that Sunday morning with preparation for the staging of a major accident. By 3 o'clock the scene was one of ruin and devastation. The double decker bus had been positioned nose-on to the train, and a hundred and forty-seven casualties had been placed inside the vehicles.

There was plenty of atmosphere. Dense clouds of steam, smoke from a burning coach, fire engine bells clanging, and shouts and moans from the trapped and injured casualties. Everyone took it seriously.

A blood-soaked trousered leg poked out of a splintered carriage door. A woman who was supposed to have been thrown through the bus roof lay unconscious in a dangerous position on the sloping roof of the train. There were few windows in the first coach which were not smashed and broken glass lay on carriage seats and floors. A screaming child climbed out of the leaning bus and ran down the railway line with blood trickling down her face from a gash on her cheek.

The briefings had been very thorough. A woman with bloodstained hair and a smashed lower leg was heard to tell a nurse that her husband would be cross because she had broken her new teeth! Passengers were worrying about each other, their children and their belongings while all the time acting the pain and disability of their injuries. The situation brought the best out of the rescuers and first aiders.

Tight-lipped firemen and Civil Defence rescue men hacked their way through the debris to reach some of the casualties. The first aiders and nurses teamed up to bandage and comfort, to carry the injured and take messages. Everyone who could drink was brought a cup of tea. The atmosphere of realism was maintained by the casualties throughout their journey by ambulance until they had been discharged from hospital. Valuable lessons were learned by casualties and workers, many of whom said afterwards, 'It was so real I forgot it was a staged exercise'.

☆ ☆ ☆

At the Gasworks

Tottenham gas works was the scene of an 'explosion' on Sunday, 15th June. It had been arranged to test the efficiency of the plans of the North London District, St. John Ambulance Brigade, speedy mobilisation in the event of a major civil disaster. Two hundred St. John personnel responded to a lunch-time call. It was a magnificent performance because without buses travel difficulties were great, but they came in from a wide area.

Dr. R. L. MacQueen, area surgeon, planned the exercise. First aiders reinforced by local Civil Defence rescue parties found casualties widely scattered. Some were trapped under trucks and twisted metal and some were half buried in heaps of coal and coke. Others were thrown free of the debris and suffered from injuries of varying severity.

Scouts from a special hospital camp at Gilwell provided a mobile first aid unit on the site. After treatment the more seriously wounded were taken by ambulance to an emergency hospital set up at St. John headquarters at Edmonton.

Casualties with minor injuries returned to the debris to be rescued more than once to provide the greatest possible tally of wounded to test the organization.

The severe cases included one requiring an emergency operation; others required stitching and yet others were prepared so that they could give 'blood' or receive a blood transfusion.

Forty-eight members from Casualties Union branches at London, British Railways (Liverpool Street), and Slough and from Study Circles at Romford and Watford provided over seventy cases.

The Area Commissioner, Dr. G. M. Shawsmith and Staff Officer R. A. Payne expressed approval of the proceedings. Many valuable lessons were learnt.

The exercise showed the value of an independent organization to provide the casualties. It left all the

A motor cyclist thrown from his machine

members of the brigade to take part in the ambulance work and enabled the exercise to be mounted as a complete surprise. The only prior warning given to members of St. John was that an exercise would take place sometime in June.

Dr. L. K. Wills and Dr. Michael Cohen of C.U., London branch collaborated with Dr. MacQueen in the preparation. R. H. Humphries of London acted as liaison with St. John.

Dr. Evans took a cine film on the event and it was hoped this would be available for showing at C.U. Conference in October, 1958.

☆ ☆ ☆

Horror Crash on Expressway

Red Dragon branch were invited by Clwyd Fire Services to provide casualties for a major motorway crash exercise, involving the fire service, ambulance and coastguards. The incident was staged on the new Llandullas bypass near Colwyn Bay, which was shortly to be opened. This was to test the strength of the emergency services should a major accident occur on it. The pile-up involved a coachload of tourists, a JCB, a chemical tanker, and four cars and a Securicor van carrying chemicals.

Fire and ambulance crews from all over Clwyd converged on the scene and were faced with the incredible sight of wrecked vehicles, dead bodies and twenty-five trapped and injured casualties. Although they knew there was going to be an exercise on the expressway, Red Dragon branch took them by surprise.

The fire brigade commanding officer, who planned the exercise, went to great lengths to collect dozens of their fire service training dummies. He made a big show of taking them down to the incident site until he had all the firemen convinced that it was them they would be rescuing. As the firemen rushed to the scene, sirens wailing (our cue to start acting), they were overheard to exclaim: 'Look those people are real, and they are bleeding!'

To add to the already rigorous task at hand, the radioactive flash in the Securicor van burst open on impact, contaminating both the driver, who was dead, and the passenger. The passenger was rushing around the scene, dazed and confused, contaminating everyone he went near, until he was marched out of the way by two firemen.

The chemical incident unit from Deeside (twenty-five miles away), was requested to attend the scene. In the meantime, the firemen had to rig up a make-shift decontamination bath (using three ladders and a tarpaulin), in which all the contaminated casualties had to be cleaned off before they could be taken away by ambulance.

While the firemen were busy coping with the dangers of contamination, the ambulance crews had their hands full dealing with a coachload of tourists, one of whom had an epileptic fit, the driver who had a heart attack, and two young girls who were vomiting. In the three other cars on the scene, there were even more headaches for the emergency services, with numerous people representing arterial bleeding, unconsciousness, fractures and cuts. The chemical tanker caused concern for a while, until the driver (who had an open Pott's fracture) assured the firemen that it was empty.

Meanwhile the coastguards, fireman and ambulance crews were kept busy down on the beach, dealing with two casualties who were in a car and had gone over the barrier and landed on its roof. The driver was trapped in the car with a fractured pelvis and had to be cut out from the vehicle. The passenger had managed to get out of the car and had wandered off in a dazed condition, only to fall down some twenty feet and land between concrete breakwaters on the shingle below. Coastguards had to climb down to her and extricate her, before they could pull her up and then search the rest of the beach for any other casualties.

The services were certainly put through a rigorous test, lasting just under two hours. They said they had learned a great deal. Red Dragon branch, with the help of members from London and Altrincham branches, certainly 'enjoyed' the incident. As an added bonus, we were all made overnight celebrities when BBC Wales gave a four minute report of the exercise on the evening news. Certain members are still being shouted at across the street, 'Hey! saw you on the tele!'

SARAH WALKER
and DAVID BUTLER

☆ ☆ ☆

The Best Laid Schemes of Mice an' Men —

At 5.30 a.m. I realized they had gone wrong. I woke to the sound of heavy rain pouring relentlessly and to the gloomy sound of our foghorn. Rain and fog for our exercise in the middle of June in the middle of our harbour!

Fortunately by 9.00 am the rain ceased, leaving only damp thick mist — Probably realistic conditions for an accident at sea, but it spoiled visibility from ship to shore and vice versa.

This exercise was planned to test the ability of the services and organizations to co-operate in an emergency — namely the engines of a fishing boat had exploded with much noise and smoke, the steering, temporarily out of control, caused the *Ocean Venture* to collide with the yacht *Stannair*. Siren and klaxon would add emphasis at 11.30 a.m. exactly, and a policeman, on the beat, would radio for assistance. He would call the police rescue team from H.Q., the inshore rescue lifeboat and the ambulance, and using his initiative, would enlist any other help available and direct the St.J.A.B. members who were cruising along Pier Road in their ambulance to the scene of the accident.

It had been easy on other occasions to arrange an exercise with St.J.A.B. or the police, but in this instance it meant a great deal more work co-ordinating the arrangements. For instance the date was fixed and then Bert discovered he had miscalculated and it no longer fitted in with his shift at work. So I had to 'phone around again and suggest the tides would be more convenient a week earlier than planned, thus playing one against another for our own ends.

Then of course we had to secure the craft on which to stage the accident. One was easy, Alice Hebden's husband was 'persuaded' to lend the *Ocean Venture* and I found the commodore of the yacht club only too intrigued and willing to take part. The inshore lifeboat and the coastguard launch would be involved automatically but what about 'transport' for the scrutineers and the press — and the photographers — and don't forget to check the tide table again and adjust for summer time, etc., etc.

There was the small matter of the explosion, without which there could be no incident. We found the 'ingredients' could not be sent by post — fortunately the repertory company began its season next day and as they needed an explosion in their opening play, agreed to bring us the gunpowder, detonator and smoke cannister! Denis Cooper did the behind-scenes work and we had a glorious explosion.

Obviously the crew of a fishing vessel must be men, but I could not raise six adult males for that date and so, once again we had to call Scarborough C.U. Group to help. Again more organization, 'phone calls (anybody got any 2p pieces?) and maps and briefings had to be sent out.

How were we to get the casualties on board without

Rescue from the Bay at Whitby

being seen by the visitors strolling along the harbourside on a Sunday morning? Fortunately we secured the loan of a large room in the Missions to Seamen which is alongside. Here we were able to make-up, hold the debriefing and even make use of the showers for the cleaning-up process. This was of tremendous benefit, even if the showers did not have locks on the doors!

We required dungarees or boiler suits as suitable gear for the crew and Dr. Lockstone suggested that it would be realistic if these could be burned! I said, 'but *of course* I mean to do this.' Have you ever tried to burn something? The particular material is reluctant to catch alight and how do you scorch two fronts, one side and one back without scorching the rest? Take it from me it's messy and I know now how the kipper feels! This achieved, I now had to burn the shirts to match the holes in the boiler suits and finally the burns had to match the holes in both!

We had four casualties aboard the yacht and six on the *Ocean Venture* and they were dealt with most efficiently by the police team and the St.J.A.B. who did the further treatment on shore and were responsible for transport to hospital, where they were received by the chief nursing officer and her staff and their condition and treatment assessed. As to treatment we had only one "fatality". Hubert is only seventy-three and so we gave him an easy injury — concussion with false teeth and vomit obstructing his airway. They improvised a magnificent stretcher for him, but forgot to clear the obstruction!

Fiona had volunteered to become hysterical and was instructed to keep it going. 'If they are firm but kind, then you may quieten down. If they leave you, especially going up the steps at the quayside, then you can start off again, but if they slap your face then you can really *go to town.*' They had obviously not read the new manual, because she was slapped hard and often. So when she got mad and walloped in return, the policeman said, 'Hey, you're hurting me'!!

Jackie, who was knocked off the yacht in the collision, wasn't missed because everyone was concerned about Jane's hand crushed between the two boats. She was found floating face downwards, at some distance from the boat and the policeman on the inshore rescue craft leant out of and said, 'Give me your hand, love, and I'll pull you in.' She says as it was freezing cold the temptation was considerable!

Still, taken all in all, it was a most successful exercise. the 'powers' were delighted and we got a lot of publicity. So successful that for the first time in our existence we have been *asked* to do another one in the harbour for R.N.L.I. Day. Makes a difference to be asked instead of *offering* to get cold, wet or just frozen.

DR. LESLEY COOPER
Leader Whitby Group, Casualties Union

☆　　☆　　☆

A letter to the editor of Casualties Union.

To get the full flavour of this exercise in Whitby Harbour, with an explosion and fire simulated on board a fishing boat, you need pictures and a story — but you

277

also need a tape recording; those shouts, moans and groans that echoed through the enveloping smoke and fog across the harbour made the firing of the coastguard maroon seem almost superfluous.

And those 'casualties'. Leave aside the undoubted expertise of the 'wounds' and watch the behaviour of the 'victims', and the authenticity which made the spectators on the harbourside hard to convince that this wasn't the real thing, becomes very evident.

There was the moment when the police squad on board the boat were just preparing the lowering of the casualty down to the R.N.L.I. inshore lifeboat, when another victim decided to jump off the other end of the boat, shrieking for help and diverting the lifeboat crew who, far from finding a grateful reception, were faced with a floundering, arm-waving female, intent on doing her best to drown herself. And on the boat was another distraction for the rescuers — a middle-aged female who insisted in getting in the way, giving advice and shouting instructions at all the wrong moments.

The prize performance must go to one young lady whose 'fit of hysteria' earned her a hard slap across the backside from a policeman, and an even harder slap across the face from another rescuer — still she kept up the act. Mind, I hear that one rescuer also suffered some little discomfort in dealing with her!

And there, in the background, with a Mona Lisa smile around her mouth, and a Machiavellian gleam in her eye, amid the smoke and fog, was Mrs. Doctor Cooper . . . !

Anonymous — not for censoring by Dr. Cooper.

A PRESSMAN

Wanted by the police

You can have some narrow squeaks serving in casualties Union. David Pearse of Beckenham, on being rescued from the first coach in the Stevenage rail disaster exercise in October, was interrogated by the police who said he closely resembled one of the young men they were looking for!

Casualty left on the railway line at Stevenage

David said that the Alsation dog with the constable was too close and too fierce for comfort! Eight people were 'arrested' for looting.

Even the doctors and staff at Lister Hospital, who were on a red alert, were getting a bit confused, for the C.U. casualties were getting mixed up with the real ones. And if you are as good at your job as were the hundred and twenty casualties involved in this exercise, it is all the more advisable to wear your C.U. badge concealed in your clothing, just in case you get the full treatment!

The Hertfordshire police, fire brigade and ambulance service wanted this exercise to test their plans to deal with a large incident. And it was so realistic that road approaches and crowds of sightseers were controlled, and even Eric Claxton, there as our observer and engineer safety officer was asked why he was there and asked to move on. It was quite an experience getting into a coach that was lying on its side, and certainly a bit nerve wracking being extricated. It meant a very early start for the members who came from branches as far away as Aylesbury, Abingdon, London, Reading, Slough and Windsor, but it was a first class affair

279

Awkward angles for entry and for rescue

from our point of view, for the Railway Executive for the Eastern Region had spared no trouble to make the staging convincing and we were fortunate that the chief medical officer in charge was our own medical adviser Dr. John S. Binning, who looked after our side too!

The publicity given to the event in the Hertfordshire papers was outstanding as you can judge by the quality of the pictures reproduced here. The *North Herts Gazette* gave it a whole page, including a most credible account by one of their young women journalists who was made-up and briefed by a C.U. instructor so that she could gain the experience of acting as a casualty.

Subsequently we read a letter in the Stevenage *Comet* from Mr. Len Aldwinckle, Superintendent of the local division of St. John and his words of appreciation and explanation are worth quoting for they show that he understands the depth of study and training needful to be a skilled 'casualty'.

'I would like to praise the work of the victims of the

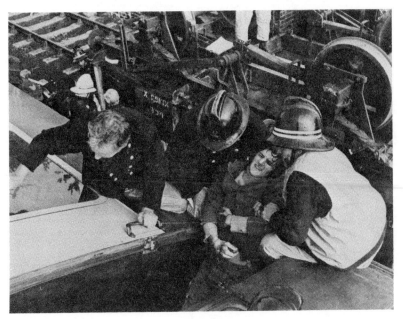

Close quarters

simulated rail crash on Sunday, 13th October. the casualties had travelled over fifty miles in the early hours, behaved in the manner that persons in a similar tragic situation would. Their injuries were made up with such realism that they could have been authentic ... The disabled person by removing an artificial limb, was able to simulate injuries involving amputation. Sometimes the casualty is badly handled and incorrectly treated but they are able to give constructive criticism to the person treating them ... I greatly appreciate their work, having treated several Casualties Union members in competitions during the last few years and feel their work should not go unnoticed by the general public, who also benefit.'

The list is almost exhaustless and we thank all those who played in any one of them most sincerely. It is in these and other ways which bring home to ordinary folks the pain and suffering that accidents

281

cause. We may persuade the world that accidents don't just happen they are caused!

61

Farewell to a Dear and Trusted Friend

With the passing of Brigadier Hugh Llewelyn Glyn Hughes, Casualties Union has lost an incomparable friend and counsellor, who, in his twenty years as president endeared himself to all our hearts. We shall miss his genial personality at our national gatherings immeasurably. The gracious presence of the president and Mrs. Hughes each year on Casualties Union Day brought a benison to the occasion that charmed guests and members alike, and smoothed away the anxieties inherent in such a large event.

The lively interest and sincere concern which Hughie showed in all the activities with which he was associated, made him occupy a place of great affection as a highly esteemed colleague. We are deeply enriched by having known him. Would that we could emulate his patience, humility and the generous way in which he gave himself to the causes in which he was involved. Though recovering from a major operation, he attended our council meeting only seven days before he died. He so often used his wide experience for the benefit of Casualties Union that it grew in stature through his influence.

His distinguished medical career encompassed two world wars in which he was awarded the D.S.O. and two bars and the M.C. He was created C.B.E. in 1945. At the time of the discovery of Belsen Concentration Camp he was D.D.M.S. Second Army and it became his primary responsibility to clean up the camp and feed, house and care for the inmates. He said the indescribable horrors of the camp were unbelievable. 'No description nor photograph could really bring home the horrors that were outside the huts, and frightful scenes inside were much worse. Within the huts there were uncountable numbers of bodies, some even in the same bunks as the living.' He gave evidence at the Belsen trial at Luneberg. In subsequent years he was invited to Israel and there he was feted as the liberator of hundreds of tortured Jews. He was shown the deep scars on the bodies of many who had survived. Lately in this country he has been working for an Anglo-Israel Society known as The Bridge in Britain.

Between the wars he was in general practice, and on his release from the Army was appointed S.A.M.O. to the S.E. Metropolitan Regional Hospital Board. In 1958 he became director of the Peckham Health Centre, and for a time was an honorary physician to the Queen. Following a period of research for the Calouste Gulbenkian Foundation he published a disturbing report on his visits to a great number of Homes for the Dying, and the appalling lack of facilities available for those elderly people suffering from terminal illnesses who were not fortunate to be nursed in their own homes. He was a foundation member of the Royal College of General Practitioners and designed the college tie (a dark green tie figured with owls because G.P.s are so frequently called out at nights!) In fact tie designing was one of his sidelines, and he is believed to have had a record of club and association ties.

One of his keenest interests was in rugby football. As a medical student he played for U.C.H. and took part in nine tours with the Barbarians. He captained United Hospitals and turned out for London, Middlesex and Devon. He became an admired and respected figure in the game and was latterly president of Barbarians and a former president of Blackheath. He died on Saturday, 24th November, 1973, suddenly and peacefully in Edinburgh, after attending the dinner following the Scottish XV v. Argentina unofficial international. He was eighty-one in July, and until quite recently enjoyed playing in competitive golf.

We share with Mrs. Hughes and his son and two daughters a deep sense of loss and sorrow at parting with our dear President, and offer them our sincere condolence.

62

We Greet a New Friend as Our President

It is with considerable uplift of heart and great pleasure that we were able to welcome to the presidency of Casualties Union a surgeon of the standing of Peter S. London, who has already shown himself to be very much 'one of us'. We hope that he will derive much interest from studying the cause and effect of accidents from the point of view of 'the mud and blood brigade', and that both he and Mrs. London will enjoy the fellowship that inevitably generates when any number of C.U. members foregather for the business or pleasure of their calling. We in turn can be assured of the wise guidance that our president will bring to our deliberations from the vast experience of accident surgery which he has built up as a consultant at the Birmingham Accident Hospital.

Here are some biographical notes provided by his wife.

A casualty himself on three occasions, Peter's choice of career can be traced back to his experience in hospital after a road accident at the age of thirteen. He was educated at King's College School, Wimbledon (School prefect, Head of House and 1st XV) and graduated M.B., B.S. with honours and distinction in surgery in 1944 at St. Thomas' Hospital Medical School, later Fellow and Hunterian Professor, F.R.C.S. (England). He is a Commander of the Order of St. John, County President of Birmingham and a member of the Medical Board.

He is the author and editor of four textbooks and

Mr Peter S. London
President 1974

numerous articles in the medical press. Chairman of the advisory council of the Head Injuries Rehabilitation Trust, and other special surgical interests include injuries of the hand, and roadside care of the victims of traffic accidents. He is a member of several government committees, particularly concerned with the ambulance services, and has a close association with the medical services of the three armed Services. The countries he has visited to lecture and advise, range from Iceland to South Africa, and from Canada to Thailand.

His interests apart from surgery (and we wonder when he ever has time for them!) include postage stamps, post office letter boxes, steam engines, church architecture and particularly stained glass. A Member of the Court of Assistants of the Worshipful Company of Glaziers, he is also interested in heraldry. None of the family, two sons and a daughter, has chosen a medical career.

Peter London's first experience of C.U. in the mass was at C.U. Day October, 1974, and following that he sent us the message printed below.

287

YOU DON'T HAVE TO BE MAD . . .

The reputation of members of Casualties Union for subjecting themselves to uncomfortable conditions not once, but time and time again, was well supported by their unflinching toleration of cold and wet weather, not to mention cold and probably wet hands at the Rugby Football Union's ground at Twickenham on Casualties Union Day, 6th October, 1974. Because your president knew something of this and was made of anything but sterner stuff he came prepared for cold, wet and mud. And what did he find? The pitch was not only lush and green but completely out of bounds and his new colleagues had a happy (and considerate) knack of suggesting coffee or finding a sheltered corner for him just as he began to feel particularly willing to get away from the chilling wind. This contrast summed up the spirit of Casualties Union. On the one hand, a complete subjection of self for the good of the cause and on the other hand a warming kindness, consideration and friendliness for all others.

What better introduction could your new president have had? In spite of Watergate and other lamentable presidential lapses the title still has some sort of aura of august formality and your preceding presidents were men of both distinction and bearing. I can claim two things in common with them — a medical qualification and, surprising though it may seem for a conscript Flight Lieutenant, the courtesy status of Brigadier on the occasion of a military surgical conference. If in due course your new president can claim any other characteristic in common with his illustrious predecessors it will be because of the generous support and encouragement of all his fellow members of Casualties Union.

PETER S. LONDON

A new start. And so to the future and hopefully to the elimination of accidents caused by the carelessness of men — yet to be written.